MARK GALLI

God wins

Heaven, Hell, and Why the Good News Is Better than *Love Wins*

Tyndale House Publishers, Inc.
Carol Stream, Illinois

Visit Tyndale online at www.tyndale.com.

TYNDALE and Tyndale's quill logo are registered trademarks of Tyndale House Publishers, Inc.

God Wins: Heaven, Hell, and Why the Good News Is Better than Love Wins

Designed by Stephen Vosloo

Published in association with James Stuart Bell at the literary agency of Whitestone Communications, Inc.

Unless otherwise indicated, all Scripture quotations are taken from the *Holy Bible*, New Living Translation, copyright © 1996, 2004, 2007 by Tyndale House Foundation. Used by permission of Tyndale House Publishers, Inc., Carol Stream, Illinois 60188. All rights reserved.

Scripture quotations marked ASV are taken from *The Holy Bible*, American Standard Version.

Scripture quotations marked NIV are taken from the Holy Bible, *New International Version,*® *NIV.*® Copyright © 1973, 1978, 1984, 2011, by Biblica, Inc.™ Used by permission of Zondervan. All rights reserved worldwide. www. zondervan.com.

Library of Congress Cataloging-in-Publication Data

Galli, Mark.
    God wins : heaven, hell, and why the Good News is better than Love wins / Mark Galli.
        p. cm.
    Includes bibliographical references (p.   ).
    ISBN 978-1-4143-6666-1 (sc)
1. Apologetics. 2. Christianity. 3. Love—Religious aspects—Christianity. 4. Bell, Rob. Love wins. I. Title.
    BT1103.G35 2011
    239—dc23   2011022665

Printed in the United States of America

17   16   15   14   13   12   11
7   6   5   4   3   2   1

To the Sunday school teacher (whose name I've long ago forgotten)

at Evangelical Free Church in Felton, California, who first taught me

at age thirteen that Jesus' words are true because Jesus said them.

Contents

Foreword

As a journalist educated at UC Santa Cruz, Fuller Seminary, and UC Davis, Mark Galli is not someone whose résumé screams "intolerant fundamentalist." Whether it's meant as a compliment or otherwise, most who know Mark would call him open minded. He doesn't rush to judgment or hastily draw lines in the sand.

Mark is a big-tent evangelical, but his penetrating critique of Rob Bell's *Love Wins* is a reminder that even a big tent can be only so big before terms such as *Bible-believing* and *evangelical*, in the historic sense, begin to lose their meaning.

Evangelical churches, both Calvinist and Arminian—while holding divergent positions on baptism, church government, and eschatology—have consistently held the common belief that everyone will go to one of two eternal destinations: heaven or hell.

As a historian and a former editor of *Christian History* magazine, Mark Galli is acutely aware of something many modern authors appear not to grasp: God hasn't given this generation—so accustomed to opinion polls that want to know what we think—the luxury of remaking theology on the fly and redefining the gospel.

Mark graciously and skillfully shows how the *Love Wins* version of the Good News is actually bad news. Our culture needs us not to reinforce its soft, malleable, and fleeting worldview but to offer a God revealed, redemptive alternative. Mark's trinitarian emphasis roots the gospel not in personal experience but in God's own nature, which is what ultimately led to his creation and redemptive plan. That's why this book is much more than a critique, and something of a manifesto.

C. S. Lewis warned against chronological snobbery—the assumption that recent viewpoints are better than ancient ones. *Love Wins* minimizes the doctrines of penal sacrifice and substitutionary atonement, ascribing them to "primitive cultures." In contrast, Galli embraces these doctrines and quotes unapologetically (and in context) Jesus and Paul, as well as Luther, Edwards, and Spurgeon. The gospel he affirms is timely precisely because it is timeless.

Mark's book is built on biblical and historical rock, not cultural sand. That's exactly the needed foundation for a response to *Love Wins*, an attractive book heavy on feelings but light on biblical and historical reasoning.

Love Wins asks hundreds of questions but offers few answers. What *God Wins* says about asking questions is worth the price of the book: "There are questions, and then there are questions." Mark Galli examines the justice questions of Job and Habakkuk, contrasting them with the self-absorbed questions of Pilate. He quotes God, who says to Job, "Who is this that questions my wisdom with such ignorant words? Brace yourself like a man, because I have some questions for you, and you must answer them" (Job 38:2-3).

Though Christ's words about hell are clear, emphatic, and repeated, our temptation is to think he didn't mean what he said. But isn't the most obvious conclusion that he really did? And that the doctrine of hell isn't a ballot measure, and God doesn't give us a vote? Hell is dreadful, but it is not evil—it's a place where evil gets punished. Something can be profoundly disturbing yet still be moral. Hell is moral because a good God must punish evil.

C. S. Lewis said of hell, "There is no doctrine which I would more willingly remove from Christianity than this, if it lay in my power. But it has the full support of Scripture and, specially, of our Lord's own words; it has always been held by Christendom; and it has the support of reason."* Dorothy Sayers, another broad-minded Christian, claimed, "We cannot repudiate Hell without altogether repudiating Christ."†

If we are free to reinterpret God's Word at will, then it is not authoritative. Christ is not authoritative. I am authoritative. My faith becomes merely a collection of fleeting opinions, always subject to revision. And that is something quite different from historic, biblically grounded Christian faith.

Love Wins argues, "God gets what he wants." Yes, but

---

* C. S. Lewis, *The Problem of Pain* (New York: Macmillan, 1962), 118.
† Dorothy Sayers, *Introductory Papers on Dante* (London: Methuen, 1954), 44.

what he wants is not limited to everyone's salvation. It also includes justice. The God revealed in Scripture is not a love-only, single-attribute God. Vital as his love is, the seraphim in his presence do not cry out day and night, "Love, love, love is the Lord God Almighty."

Love—as moderns narrowly define it—doesn't win. Rather, as Mark's title so aptly puts it, God wins. And not just any God, but the true God. The Father who is both loving and righteous, the Son who is full of both grace and truth, the merciful Spirit who has the word *Holy* in his very name. God's attributes aren't a menu from which we may choose only what we wish—he is all that he is, all the time.

The issues underlying both *Love Wins* and *God Wins* are, in the end, far bigger than hell. If we can still claim to be Bible believers while radically reinterpreting Christ's words about hell, stripping them of their straightforward meaning, why should it end there? What about Christ's virgin birth? His physical resurrection? His deity? What about moral issues? Why not reject everything we can't figure out? And what would someone have to reject, short of the very existence of God or his Son, in order to no longer be an evangelical Christian?

If the orthodox views on salvation and damnation are up for grabs, then surely virtually everything in the Apostles' Creed is also. Evangelicalism may survive attacks from the outside, but it faces the impending sinkhole of inner erosion. That's why I believe *God Wins* offers help not just for the issues of hell and universalism but also for many other issues the church is already facing, or inevitably will.

This all has profound implications about what it means to speak on behalf of God. Our job is not to be God's public relations manager or make him popular. The Almighty doesn't need us to give him a face-lift and airbrush his image. "But surely it isn't bad to try to make God look good, is it?" The question is, look good on whose terms? God has his own terms. Our task is not to help people see God favorably but to see him accurately. God has the power to touch hearts and draw people to his love and grace while they fully affirm his holiness and justice. It's not either/or but both/and.

God has appointed us to faithfully deliver his message, not to compose and edit it. He has already written the message—it's called the Bible. Who are we to spin it and tame it, or presume to be more loving than Jesus, who with outrageous love took upon himself the horrific penalty for our sin?

God's position is already taken; we need not apply. We do not own the Christian faith. It isn't ours to revise. God's Word wasn't entrusted to us so we could give it away piecemeal, leaving the next generation with the leftovers. If we go on decade after decade parceling out fragments of the faith, what will be left? When we abandon truths Christians once died for, will we no longer have truths worth living for?

Mark Galli clearly grasps the miracle that God's amazing grace delivers us from the hell we deserve. God can and will bridge the gap between himself and people, not through our doctrinal revisionism but through his sovereign grace.

I love the fact that *God Wins* doesn't discourage honest questions but calls on us to go to God's Word for honest answers. Mark encourages us to recognize the mysteries of God and respectfully bow our knees to his divine authority.

I pray you'll read this book with the knowledge that our churches are at a doctrinal and leadership crossroads, and much is at stake. If our sins aren't big enough to warrant eternal punishment, then perhaps the grace God showed us on the cross isn't big enough to warrant eternal praise. (God forbid that we should believe this.)

We are sometimes tempted to shrink God so he fits inside the borders of our minds. But those are small borders, and he is a big God. There is great comfort in knowing a God who loves me but doesn't need my counsel. The best part about *God Wins*, from my perspective, is that as I read it, God became greater and I became less.

Randy Alcorn

Introduction

IN RECENT MONTHS, a new book has captured the attention of people around the world. In churches and book groups and countless blog posts, folks have been talking about *Love Wins*. Some are intrigued by it; others are infuriated. Whether readers agree with some of it, most of it, or little of it, nearly everyone has a strong opinion about the book. At the very least, it has prompted many Christians to think more deeply about what they believe.

Love Wins is definitely a provocative book. The concept of love winning isn't a new insight, but author Rob Bell has a gift for helping us hear it afresh. And he's right as far as that message goes: love *does* win. But, of course, that depends on what you mean by the word *love*. And it depends on what you mean by *wins*. As arresting as that title phrase is, it simply doesn't go far enough. As we dig deeper into God's Word, we discover it is less important that love wins than that God wins. The purpose of this book is to explain that crucial difference.

Lyrical Preaching

The fact that so many people are talking about *Love Wins* is a great development. In one of the two great commandments of Jesus, he instructs us to love God with our minds.[1] Sparked by this book, thousands of Christians are pondering anew many of the great teachings of the Christian faith. Some who previously thought theology dry and dull have discovered, along with novelist and Christian apologist and writer Dorothy Sayers, that "the dogma is the drama." And maybe most important, we are rediscovering how crucial theology truly is for the life of the church.

The pastor of a popular megachurch that attracts thousands of people each weekend, Rob Bell is a dynamic and effective communicator. He asks pointed questions that prompt people to think, and he has an instinct for the questions people are already asking. When he starts talking about God's love or the power of the Resurrection, few can match his dynamism. This is one reason *Love Wins* has taken off and quickly landed on the *New York Times* bestseller list.

Love Wins gives readers reason to reexamine the story of Jesus. It sets that story in its largest context, but without minimizing its individual dimension. Rob Bell says it's true that Jesus came to die on the cross so we can have a relationship with God. "But . . . for the first Christians," he says, "the story was, first and foremost, bigger, grander. More massive. . . . God has inaugurated a movement in Jesus's resurrection to renew, restore, and reconcile everything." Later he adds, "A gospel that leaves out its cosmic scope will always feel small."[2]

Indeed.

In another passage *Love Wins* waxes eloquent about the grace of God in ways the great champion of grace Martin Luther would have resonated with. The book says the Good News

> begins with the sure and certain truth that we are loved.
>
> That in spite of whatever has gone horribly wrong deep in our hearts
> and has spread to every corner of the world,
> in spite of our sins,
> failures,
> rebellion,
> and hard hearts,
> in spite of what's been done to us or what we've done,
> God has made peace with us.
> Done. Complete.
> As Jesus said, "It is finished."[3]

And the book ends with a plea no evangelical could argue with:

> May you experience this vast,
> expansive, infinite, indestructible love

that has been yours all along. . . .
And may you know,
deep in your bones,
that love wins.[4]

These and many other such passages are true to the gospel and beautiful in their execution. Certainly, there is common theological ground to be found in this book. But it doesn't paint the entire picture of the gospel.

Questions and Confusion

The discussion in *Love Wins* is peppered with numerous questions. And not just any questions, but questions that get at the heart of some of the most theologically troubling issues in the Christian faith. Take just one that is raised at the very beginning of the book:

Of all the billions of people who have ever lived,
will only a select number "make it to a better place"
and every single other person suffer in torment
and punishment forever? Is this acceptable to God?
Has God created millions of people over tens of
thousands of years who are going to spend eternity
in anguish? Can God do this, or even allow this, and
still claim to be a loving God?[5]

Who among us hasn't pondered such questions, if not with friends or in church, in the middle of the night as we stare up at the ceiling, unable to sleep?

At other points in *Love Wins*, the reader is assaulted with the seeming contradictions of Scripture. Other times the book raises questions in a way that suggests that no thinking, compassionate person could possibly believe such nonsense. But whatever tone the book takes, it always seems to get at questions that are at the core of our biblical faith.

Unfortunately, Bell's answers are difficult to grasp. Though a compelling communicator, he can be equally as mystifying at times. Some of his arguments lack coherence, and at times no real resolution is sought.

It is true that there will always be unanswered questions when we think about the deeper issues of faith. The Bible is a book full of mystery and wonder. If we find we have created a doctrine of God that makes perfect sense to us, then we're probably no longer talking about the God of the Bible. We are finite and sinful; he is infinite and holy. There are aspects of God's being that we won't ever be able to grasp. We can only say with Paul,

Who can know the Lord's thoughts?
Who knows enough to give him advice?
And who has given him so much
that he needs to pay it back?

For everything comes from him and exists by his power
and is intended for his glory. All glory to him forever!
Amen.

(ROMANS 11:34-36)

That being said, there are many issues on which the Bible is much clearer than *Love Wins* lets on. The book does not do justice to the Bible's grand narrative; it is simply not an adequate reflection of the historic Christian faith that has been taught through the centuries. At points, *Love Wins* gets close to grasping the immensity of the Good News, but it never quite gets there. It's like a football team driving down the field and settling for a field goal instead of scoring a touchdown.

Great News

I need to be clear up front about one thing. This is not a book about Rob Bell or Rob Bell's theology. (That is why in referring to ideas in the book, I do so in terms of what *Love Wins* says, not what Rob Bell believes.) This is a book that uses *Love Wins* as a starting point to talk about key theological issues we as a church and as individuals are thinking about today.

My goal is not to merely wrestle with *Love Wins* and the questions it raises. I want to place those questions in a larger biblical context. In the end, I want this book to be a call back to the Good News, which in my view is even better than "love wins." I'd like to invite you to immerse yourself in a gospel that is richer, deeper, and more amazing than we often imagine.

—Mark Galli

CHAPTER 1

The Really Important Question

THERE ARE QUESTIONS, and then there are questions.

In *Love Wins*, there are lots of questions—eighty-six in the first chapter alone. The book you are currently reading will address a number of them, because they are good questions. But before that, the first thing we need to do is think about the very nature of questions. Because there are questions, and then there are *questions*.

There are questions like the one Mary, the mother of Jesus, asks the angel when he tells her some astounding news. Mary is a young woman engaged to marry Joseph when the angel Gabriel appears to her.

"Greetings, favored woman!" he bursts out. "The Lord is with you!"

Suddenly finding herself in the presence of a messenger of God, Mary is naturally "confused and disturbed."

"Don't be afraid, Mary," Gabriel reassures her, "for you have found favor with God!"

And then he drops the bombshell: "You will conceive and give birth to a son, and you will name him Jesus." This Jesus, he says, will be very great, will be called the Son of the Most High, will be given the throne of his ancestor David, and will reign over Israel forever in a Kingdom that will never end.

That's a lot to take in. Most mothers just want to know they'll have a baby with all ten fingers and ten toes. But what exactly all this means—Son of the Most High? ruler like King David? reign forever?—seems not as perplexing to Mary as one other detail. "But how can this happen?" she asks. "I am a virgin."

That's her question, and it's a good one. A virgin getting pregnant without the help of a man—well, this sort of thing doesn't happen every day. It's an honest question, prompted by natural curiosity and driven, not by fear and doubt, but by wonder: how is God going to pull this off?

Mary asked one type of question; the other type was posed by Zechariah a few months earlier. A priest married to Mary's cousin Elizabeth, Zechariah was an old man at the other end of life and the reproduction cycle when the angel Gabriel appeared to him (see Luke 1:5-23).

It happened in the Temple, as Zechariah burned incense in the sanctuary. Suddenly an angel of the Lord appeared before him. "Zechariah was shaken and overwhelmed with fear," Luke's Gospel says.

"Don't be afraid, Zechariah!" Gabriel reassures. "God has heard your prayer."

What prayer? For a son? For Elijah to come to herald the Messiah? For the Messiah to come? We're not told what Zechariah's prayer had been, only that it has been heard. This is what Gabriel told him: Zechariah and Elizabeth would have a son whom they were to name John, and this John would be an extraordinary man.

Again, Gabriel piles on the attributes. John will be great in the eyes of the Lord, will be filled with the Holy Spirit—even before his birth—will turn many Israelites to the Lord, will be a man with the spirit and power of Elijah, will prepare people for the coming of the Lord, will turn the hearts of the fathers to their children, and will cause the rebellious to accept godly wisdom.

Again, that's a lot to take in. And the thing that bothers Zechariah is the thing that bothers Mary: biology. "How can I be sure this will happen?" he asks the angel. "I am an old man now, and my wife is also well along in years."

His question seems like a logical one. But it is not a good question. Gabriel chastises Zechariah, telling him in no uncertain terms that he, Gabriel, stands in the very presence of God. Of course God can deliver on this promise of good news!

"Since you didn't believe what I said," Gabriel continues, "you will be silent and unable to speak until the child is born." The consequence for asking a bad question: Zechariah is made mute. No more questions. Only silence.

So what's the difference here? The questions are so similar. Why is Mary's treated with respect while Zechariah's is an occasion for spiritual discipline? Why does the angel seem indifferent to Mary's natural curiosity and angry about Zechariah's?

The difference appears in one little additional clause Zechariah adds to his question. Mary simply asks, "How can this happen?" Zechariah asks, "How can *I be sure* this will happen?"

Mary's question is about God. Zechariah's question is about himself.

Mary's question assumes God will do something good and great, and seeks to know how it will unfold. Zechariah is not at all sure that God is good and great, and seeks proof.

Mary wants to learn more about the goodness of God. Zechariah mostly wants to be self-assured.

As I said, there are questions, and then there are questions.

As these two stories show, questions driven by faith and questions driven by self-justification can sound very similar. Sometimes they can be identical in their wording, but they are not identical in their motives. A question can be grounded in trust in God's goodness—or it can be a demand for a sign. God is pleased with the former, but not so pleased with the latter.

As Jesus put it, "Only an evil, adulterous generation would demand a miraculous sign" (Matthew 16:4). The demand for signs is a demand for proof. It's a clue that the heart is not right. It's putting God on trial. We don the judge's robes and climb into the judicial bench, looking down at the accused.[6]

The problem with requests for signs is that they mask unbelief—and ultimately they become an attempt to justify a lack of faith. Such is the case with the theologian described in Luke 10, whose questions prompt Jesus to tell the parable of the Good Samaritan. Asked how one gains eternal life, Jesus answers clearly, but the theologian only asks another question because, as Luke notes, "the man wanted to justify his actions" (verse 29).

Questions driven by a demand for signs never cease—and they never satisfy. The unfortunate conclusion in the Gospel of John is, "Despite all the miraculous signs Jesus had done, most of the people still did not believe in him" (John 12:37).

The point is that questions are not just questions. There is no such thing as a neutral inquiry when it comes to questions about God.

Love Wins is a book running over with questions. In chapter 1, we are presented with questions like

Does God punish people for thousands of years with infinite, eternal torment for things they did in their few finite years of life?

Is there really no hope for someone who dies an atheist?

Is the salvation of others dependent on what we do—that is, our ability to send missionaries to them?

And that's just the beginning. No question asked in *Love Wins* is actually new. Many questions raised in the book were asked in the Bible. But we certainly feel the force of the questions in a new way today.

No matter the questions, here's the point: for some, these questions arise out of a trusting faith. For others, they arise out of a desire to have God prove himself on human terms.

We can't tell which is which simply by listening to the question. What drives the question resides in the human heart. We cannot judge anyone else because we cannot see into their hearts. But when we start asking questions of God, we can look into our own hearts. And we can ask ourselves a couple of hard questions. First, why am I asking these questions? Second, are they grounded in God's goodness or in a desire to justify myself?

Sometimes the answers to these self-directed questions are obvious. Sometimes they are not. Most of the time it's a mix. But given human nature—the heart is desperately wicked, according to Jeremiah 17:9—we can safely assume that the questions are largely driven by a desire to justify ourselves, to put God in the dock, and to don those judicial robes.

This does not mean we don't have any legitimate questions. It does not mean that we are forbidden to ask God anything. God is not threatened by our questions. But when we start asking questions, we are called to begin with a prayer grounded in repentance and humility.

As in, "Lord, help me overcome my unbelief."

Or, even more crucial, "O God, be merciful to me . . . a sinner."

As James says, "You don't have what you want because you don't ask God for it. And even when you ask, you don't get it because your motives are all wrong" (4:2-3).

So before we ask our questions, we are wise to pray for both help and mercy that we will learn to ask with the right spirit.

You Call That an Answer?

People have been asking hard questions since biblical days. But some of those questions have also been answered. Let's note two of them, and how God answered. It will help us see what we're up against when we start asking tough questions of the Creator of heaven and earth.

One example comes from the little-read book of Habakkuk. It was written during the brutal Babylonian conquest of Jerusalem. This spawned a plethora of violence and injustice, leading to various forms of human misery. When Habakkuk had seen enough, he started to interrogate God:

> *How long, O LORD, must I call for help?*
> *But you do not listen!*
> *"Violence is everywhere!" I cry,*
> *but you do not come to save.*
> *Must I forever see these evil deeds?*
> *Why must I watch all this misery?*

Wherever I look,
  I see destruction and violence.
I am surrounded by people
  who love to argue and fight.
The law has become paralyzed,
  and there is no justice in the courts.
The wicked far outnumber the righteous,
  so that justice has become perverted.

  (HABAKKUK 1:2-4)

After God tells him that because of the sins of his people, things may actually get worse, Habakkuk questions whether the punishment fits the crime:

O LORD my God, my Holy One, you who are eternal—
  surely you do not plan to wipe us out?
O LORD, our Rock, you have sent these Babylonians
    to correct us,
  to punish us for our many sins.
But you are pure and cannot stand the sight of evil.
  Will you wink at their treachery?
Should you be silent while the wicked
  swallow up people more righteous than they?

  (HABAKKUK 1:12-13)

Or to put it as we might today, in light of all the suffering around us, how can God be just? God's answer to Habakkuk is this:

Write my answer plainly on tablets,
*   so that a runner can carry the correct message to others.*
This vision is for a future time.
*   It describes the end, and it will be fulfilled.*
If it seems slow in coming, wait patiently,
*   for it will surely take place.*

(HABAKKUK 2:2-3)

In other words, "I'll take care of the Babylonians in my time. It will all work out in the end. Be patient."

The answer to Habakkuk's cry is to be patient? Is that the type of thing a compassionate God tells his anguished people? Apparently. And it's an answer that Habakkuk accepts at face value: "I have heard all about you, LORD," he says. "I am filled with awe by your amazing works. . . . I will wait quietly for the coming day when disaster will strike the people who invade us" (Habakkuk 3:2, 16).

None of Job's Business

As another example, take the champion questioner of God in the Old Testament, Job. He certainly seems to have the right to complain. He has lost his home, his children, his livestock, and his health—everything that was a blessing is gone, and now his life is nothing but a curse. And why? Job can't spot a single thing he did to deserve his fate. So he cries out to God:

Why wasn't I born dead?
*   Why didn't I die as I came from the womb? . . .*

Why wasn't I buried like a stillborn child,
like a baby who never lives to see the light?
(JOB 3:11, 16)

Oh, why give light to those in misery,
and life to those who are bitter?
They long for death, and it won't come.
They search for death more eagerly than for hidden
treasure.
They're filled with joy when they finally die,
and rejoice when they find the grave.
Why is life given to those with no future,
those God has surrounded with difficulties?
(JOB 3:20-23)

Job pummels God with question after question after question—until God shows up and queries his accuser:

Who is this that questions my wisdom
with such ignorant words?
Brace yourself like a man,
because I have some questions for you,
and you must answer them.
(JOB 38:2-3)

That's the beginning of an onslaught of divine questions for Job:

Where were you when I laid the foundations of the earth?
Tell me, if you know so much.

(JOB 38:4)

Who kept the sea inside its boundaries
as it burst from the womb,
and as I clothed it with clouds
and wrapped it in thick darkness?

(JOB 38:8-9)

Have you given the horse its strength
or clothed its neck with a flowing mane?
Did you give it the ability to leap like a locust?
Its majestic snorting is terrifying!

(JOB 39:19-20)

And then the clincher question, which leaves Job dumbfounded:

Will you discredit my justice
and condemn me just to prove you are right?

(JOB 40:8)

This is not a very empathetic response. Looks as though God could take a few lessons in grief counseling. But Job tells us that, finally, he is able to trust God.

You asked, "Who is this that questions my wisdom with
such ignorance?"
It is I—and I was talking about things I knew nothing
about,
things far too wonderful for me. . . .
I take back everything I said,
and I sit in dust and ashes to show my repentance.

(J O B   42:3, 6)   .

What we see in these two incidents is that God seems relatively unconcerned with giving specific answers to the anguished questions of Habakkuk and Job. He answers them, but not point for point. This suggests that all our questions about God's wisdom and justice and love may not be all that important to God in the end—or at least not as important as other things.

This doesn't mean we can't ask them. In Christ, we have the freedom to speak what's on our hearts and minds. God isn't going to cast us from his presence because we ask him some tough questions. It just means that we shouldn't take our questions too seriously, because apparently God doesn't take them too seriously.

It may shock us to hear it put that way. We think pretty highly of ourselves and our questions. We think it's our right to ask such questions and to demand such answers, even from God. But God does not seem to share this view. In the Bible, whenever God is asked a question that throws into doubt his kindness or justice, he more or less refuses to answer. In some instances he says, "You have no idea what you are talking about." Or he says, "You'll get an answer in my good time."

Jesus' Big Question

Indeed, there is a deep mystery when it comes to our questions—and yet a deep *mercy*.

All our uncertainties about God's justice and love are summed up in a single question, the one Jesus asks on our behalf as he hangs from the cross: "My God, my God, why have you forsaken me?" In this question, all our anguished questions about God's goodness come together.

Does God forsake us? Is he indifferent to our suffering? Can he be trusted?

Jesus, representing us on the cross, as true man, is asking all that and more on our behalf.

And God's response?

Silence.

When God hears this question, a question that examines his very goodness, he does not strike back or walk away in disgust. He simply absorbs the question in loving silence. And when our questions require his forgiveness, that forgiveness is available to cover every question we've ever asked or will ever ask, especially those questions that are nothing but a demand for a sign or an attempt to justify ourselves.

While Jesus as true man is asking the question behind all our questions—Can God be trusted to be good and just?— Jesus as true God is answering that question with another: "Can you trust and love the God who will die for you?"

As the Cross demonstrates, God takes us seriously. He takes our sin seriously. But he continues to show relative indifference to our questions. He does not answer them to our intellectual satisfaction; he refuses to submit himself to our interrogations.

That's because the really important question in the Bible is not any question we ask of God but the question he asks of us. And though it is appropriate to ponder any number of questions—for this is part of what it means to love God with all our minds—*our* questions must always take a backseat.

They take a backseat to the prayer for faith and mercy, not to mention the illumination of the Holy Spirit.

And they take a backseat to the only question that really matters: "Who do you say I am?" (Matthew 16:15).

The answer to that question is revealed on the cross. And until we embrace this answer, none of our questions even make sense, none of the questions raised in *Love Wins* can be properly addressed, and none of the answers the Bible supplies will satisfy. Until we comprehend who God is, all our questions are like chasing after the wind.

So let's see how the Bible talks about this God.

CHAPTER 2

Who Is This God?

IT IS ONE of the most interesting conversations recorded in Scripture.

Jesus has just been arrested, and he stands before the Roman governor, Pilate. Pilate wants to know if Jesus is guilty of the charges made against him; that is, whether Rome has any interest in the case. So Pilate begins with the most important question a Roman governor would need answered. He turns to Jesus and asks, "Are you the king of the Jews?"

If Jesus is king of the Jews, then Pilate's job is pretty simple: execute Jesus. No Roman governor is going to show mercy when it comes to insurrection. But in his usual way, Jesus turns the question around. What began as a discussion of urgent and practical matters of state turns to matters eternal and heavenly. Jesus has a way of doing that when we start asking questions we think are so important. He replies, "Is this your own question, or did others tell you about me?" (John 18:34).

In other words, "Is this question about me, or is it about you? Are you really interested in who I am, or are you just interested in solving a problem and moving on?" Jesus knows that many of the questions we pose are not really about him, but about us. Often we're merely using Jesus to justify ourselves or to make ourselves feel better about rejecting him.

For his part, Pilate admits that Jesus doesn't really concern him and that the only reason he's even talking to Jesus is because the Jewish leaders need his permission for an execution.

That's when Jesus finally gets around to explaining what type of king he is: "My Kingdom is not an earthly kingdom. If it were, my followers would fight to keep me from being handed over to the Jewish leaders. But my Kingdom is not of this world" (John 18:36). In other words, "You needn't worry yourself about me. I'm not the type of king who is going to cause you political problems."

Then Pilate asks, "So you are a king?"

Pilate is naturally confused. It's likely he never considered that a person could be a king but not a political king. He suspects that this Jesus really doesn't concern him, but he needs to make sure.

Jesus replies, "You say I am a king. Actually, I was born

and came into the world to testify to the truth. All who love the truth recognize that what I say is true" (John 18:37).

To this, Pilate replies, "What is truth?" And he ends the conversation.

What exactly Pilate meant by this final question has been the subject of much speculation through the centuries. But it seems to me that Pilate is asking the central question of human life—a really good question—but he's asking it in a cynical way. It's as if he's saying, "Oh, so this is about philosophy, about religion, about the search for truth. Well, that's not something that anyone can really answer, is it? It's certainly not something a Roman governor has to know before he can effectively rule." So he skeptically tosses the question, not bothering to hear what Jesus might have to say in response. He immediately returns to the people who brought Jesus to him in the first place.

Those of us who read this passage today clearly see why John, the writer of this Gospel, included this conversation in his work. When Pilate asks, "What is truth?" our minds immediately go back to a statement Jesus made earlier in the Gospel, a statement that reverberates again in this conversation: "I am the way, the truth, and the life. No one can come to the Father except through me" (John 14:6).

The irony here is that, though Pilate fails to stick around for the answer, the answer has already been given. And in a few hours, the answer will be explained. What is truth? Truth is the God who so despises sin that he judges it for the evil it is. Truth is the God who offers the forgiveness of sins to all.

Truth is the God who so loves the world that he gives his only Son. And as the end of the last chapter notes, it is only when we can discern the truth of who God is that we can put our questions into proper perspective.

Unfortunately, this preliminary work is not done in *Love Wins*. We are met with an onslaught of questions, most of which are not answered. Several answers are attempted, some more successfully than others. In fact, many answers revolve around the loving character of God. But because the book never explains the nature and degree of that love, the idea of love in *Love Wins* tends to comes across as beautiful and exciting—but ultimately thin and sentimental. It does not communicate the gravity, the thickness, the mystery of God.

So we need to look in some depth—as much depth as a chapter allows—to begin to get at the truth of God.

God the Creator, Lord, and Lawgiver

Just before Jesus goes to the cross, he shows us what type of God we are dealing with. He reveals something extraordinary about God the Father, about himself, and about us. That's not a bad place to begin thinking about who this God who calls us to love and trust him really is. But before we look at how Jesus describes God's essence, let's take a look at two alternate ways we tend to think about God the Father, which will help us see how extraordinary Jesus' description is.

Many people who want to understand God begin at what they think is the beginning: "In the beginning God created the heavens and the earth" (Genesis 1:1). They start by talking about God as Creator. This naturally moves them to start talking about God as Lord, for God is indeed Lord of his creation. And that leads them to talk about God as Lord of our lives, as Lawgiver. For our Creator creates laws by which his creation is to live.

When we begin with God the Creator, we begin with God as a transcendent authority. With a God who sits above us in the heavens. With a God who stands over us as Lord. He commands and we obey. As the Bible notes in Genesis 3, this relationship became rocky right from the start because we did not obey this Lord. We sinned. That sin led to death. And that death was and is inevitable for all.

The Creator God is also, of course, a gracious God. So he makes it possible for us to be forgiven. He sent Jesus to the cross to die for our sins, to settle the score between us and God. The resulting good news is that we are forgiven! This is good news indeed. And Christians are right to rejoice in this news daily.

But we're still relating first and foremost to a Creator. A Lord. A Lawgiver. And while we are grateful for his gracious forgiveness, this does not necessarily prompt us to love this God. We experience relief, yes. Thanksgiving, yes. But love? Maybe, maybe not.

We can see how this plays out in our daily lives. My boss asks me to get a project done by a certain date. Because I fail to manage my time well—let's face it, I was lazy—I don't meet the deadline. I walk into his office and make excuses, but in the end I just admit I blew it. My boss says, "Okay, all is forgiven. Let's move on." I am extremely grateful! I walk out on cloud nine, relieved I still have a job and still have a relationship with a boss. But I don't particularly love my boss more. He's still my boss. A good boss, a forgiving boss. But a boss.

That's the way it can be when we think of God mostly as Creator, as Lord, as Lawgiver. He is an authority figure who demands obedience yet offers forgiveness. But he's not necessarily someone we automatically want to love.

Let me be clear. God is Creator. He is Lord. He is Lawgiver. These are not just add-ons to his nature. They are not outdated ways of thinking about him. It's just that, according to Jesus, they are not what God is at the center of his being.

It's only at the center of God's being that we can begin to understand God the Creator, the Lord, and the Lawgiver.

God the Agent

Another way people picture God is as Agent. This is not a biblical word, but it is clearly a biblical idea. God is the one who gets things done on our behalf.

This is the primary characteristic of God described in *Love Wins*. God is often described as being love, but in the end, the book's depiction of love is nearly always as a feeling we enjoy or something God has done for us.

No question, God has done a lot! He has created us. He

has given us gifts and talents, family and friends, meaningful work. He has forgiven us. He has given us eternal life, which can be enjoyed even today, as well as the promise of a heaven that is even more real than we can imagine. In short, as the book says over and over, he has given us the possibility of experiencing peace, joy, and love forever.

Let's just look at one example of this in the chapter entitled "The Good News Is Better than That."

Here the Good News

> begins with the sure and certain truth that we are
> loved.
> That in spite of whatever has gone horribly
> wrong deep in our hearts
> and has spread to every corner of the world,
> in spite of our sins,
> failures,
> rebellion,
> and hard hearts,
> in spite of what's been done to us or what we've
> done,
> God has made peace with us.
> Done. Complete.
> As Jesus said, "It is finished."[7]

If this isn't good news, I don't know what is. This is a marvelous summary of God as Agent.

But is this good news good enough? Does it probe deeply

enough? Does it express the best news the Bible proclaims? Not quite. Because it's only about God as Agent. Someone who accomplishes something *for* us, as well as something that God does *to* us. Thus, according to *Love Wins*, life in God is about "stillness, peace, and that feeling of your soul being at rest." The gospel is about having "experienced" the Resurrection and having "tapped into the joy" of the universe. It is about being "free from guilt and fear and the terrifying, haunting, ominous voice" of condemnation. In short, it's about an exhilarating experience.[8]

In *Love Wins*, life in God is also about us doing stuff for God and for others. It's about being "partners" with Jesus and being "passionate about participating in the ongoing creation of the world." And it's about "asking things, learning things, creating things, and sharing it all with others who are finding the same kind of joy."[9]

God as Agent. Someone who makes it possible for us to do life to its fullest.

Love Wins is not the only place we find this as the primary way of thinking about God. This is the same God who is talked about and preached and praised in nearly all our services and books and songs. This is the God we're excited to know about.

But when this view of God stands at the beginning and the center of our understanding—well, it creates some insurmountable problems.

For one, it inevitably makes the Christian life about *us*. It's about what God has done for *us*. What *we* experience as a result. What *we* do in response. This problem is pandemic in evangelical Christianity. And unfortunately, *Love Wins* just reinforces this bad theological habit. Despite its occasional line that suggests that the really important thing is God, the overwhelming emphasis in the book is on our experience and our doing. The same is true of the evangelical church. There is the periodic reminder that it's all about God and what he has done on the Cross, but on a day-to-day basis, the Christian faith is mostly about us.

This has been noted in many recent articles and books, such as Michael Horton's *Christless Christianity* and Phillip Cary's *Good News for Anxious Christians: 10 Practical Things You Don't Have to Do*. We market the gospel as something that can give people hope, joy, and purpose—as an experience God will give us. We think of the Christian life in terms of how God will transform our lives or how we'll work with God to transform the world—so we will be better people and the world will be a better place. We look to God to encounter us personally so that he will seem real to us—so we will feel spiritual. It's mostly about God the Agent, who makes our happiness possible to an eternal degree.

I don't want to disparage all this, because as far as it goes, it is pretty good news. God does marvelous things in our lives. But this is not the gospel. When we talk about God in this way, it leaves us trapped in self. And unfortunately, at the end of *Love Wins*, the line used to sum it up is pretty much the mantra for our Christian lives: "May *you experience* this vast, expansive, infinite, indestructible love."[10]

That's one problem with God as Agent being the controlling idea. The other is this: when God is primarily our Agent, he remains separate from us. He does things for us. He does things to us. We do things for him. God is there for us, but ultimately only over there.

When Jesus talks about God, he makes sure we know that God is our Agent and our Creator. But he also wants us to know something more.

God the Lover

If God is not primarily a Creator and Lord, and not primarily an Agent working on our behalf, who does Jesus think God is?

As Jesus prepares to face death, he prays for his disciples. In his prayer he reveals something surprising about God. At the end of his petition, he says this:

> *I am in them and you are in me. May they experience such perfect unity that the world will know that you sent me and that you love them as much as you love me. Father, I want these whom you have given me to be with me where I am. Then they can see all the glory you gave me because you loved me even before the world began!*
>
> (JOHN 17:23-24)

There is a lot going on here, to say the least. So I will set aside a discussion of the corporate nature of salvation; that is, how Jesus' followers are one. What I want us to notice here is the relationship between Jesus and his Father, and between the Father and us.

The first thing we note is that God is first and foremost a Lover. "You loved me even before the world began," Jesus says to his Father. Love is something God has been participating in for a really long time.

God is indeed a Creator, but there wasn't always a creation. God is Lord of and Lawgiver for humankind, but there wasn't always a humanity that needed law. God is Agent of all that is good in our lives, but there was a time when we did not exist and there was no need for an Agent. As crucial as it is to know that God is Creator, Lord, and Agent, this is not who God has been from the very beginning—if we can speak about God in such chronological terms! From the beginning, and in his very essence, God is love.

This does not mean that God is a warm, fuzzy emotion. Or that his love is defined by our feeling accepted despite our shortcomings. Nor is this love exhausted by the idea that God is forgiving or merciful. No, before he had anyone to accept despite their shortcomings, before he had anyone to forgive, before he needed to be merciful, God was already loving.

Specifically, God loved his Son, Jesus Christ. And his Son loved him. (It's not mentioned in this passage, but the love between the Father and the Son is shared in and with the Holy Spirit. The vital role of the Holy Spirit will be discussed in future chapters. For now the focus will be on the love between the Father and the Son.)

What does this love consist of? Well, we're dealing with the internal life of the eternal Trinity, so there will be a lot of mystery left at the end of the day. But this much Jesus reveals: "I pray that they will all be one, just as you and I are one—as you are in me, Father, and I am in you" (John 17:21).

The love between the Father and the Son is characterized by an intimate unity. Unity of will. Unity of persons. Unity of desire. Unity of being. As much as we can fathom what this means for the Father and Son, that's what their love consists of.

One way to conceive of this unity is to think of what it's like to be on a team that has just won a championship. At that moment we know an exhilarating sense of unity. All the sweat, toil, and practice; all the setbacks and arguments; all the rivalries fade into oblivion. All we're absolutely sure of for those brief, euphoric moments is that we are a *team*. We know an extraordinary unity. And that's why when a microphone is stuck in the face of one of the champions, one of the first things the athlete will say is, "I love all these guys."

This love that Jesus and the Father share is the love Jesus wants for the disciples: "I am in them and you are in me." Did you catch what Jesus is saying about love here? It flies by so quickly we're apt to miss it. So let's break it down.

First, Jesus is in the Father and the Father is in Jesus. They have such unity that theologians say that though they are two "persons," they are one being. That's love. Jesus says that he is similarly *in us*. Not exactly the same, but very close to the same. Next, Jesus is true God and true man. He is one being with us as man. He is one being with his Father as God. And in the miracle of his incarnation, his death, and his resurrection, he makes us one with the Father. Jesus is one with the Father, so now in Jesus we, too, are one with the Father.

It's as if Jesus brings us into the presence of the Father and says, "Meet your new son. Meet your new daughter." And it's as if the Father replies, "Of course!" and welcomes us with the same warm embrace he gave Jesus when everyone walked into the room. We are now part of the family.

Like all illustrations, this one falls far short of explaining the full depth of what Jesus is describing here. But the point is this: just as Jesus enjoys an intimacy with the Father—an intimacy that goes way back—now we enjoy that intimacy from this point on. As Jesus puts it at the end of this prayer, "I have revealed you to them, and I will continue to do so. Then your love for me will be in them, and I will be in them" (John 17:26).

To put it simply: to participate in the love of God means to participate in the very life of the Trinity. This is not unlike having a "personal relationship with Jesus," but it's so much more. It's personal, but it's closer and better than a mere one-on-one relationship. And as I'll explain later, it is also participation as a community of believers in the "community" of God.

It's important to note here that we are not swallowed up in divinity, as some Eastern religions maintain. As Jesus puts it, God in us, we in God. A real relationship, in a unity we can hardly imagine. With God, the God who existed before the world began. The God whose glory fills the skies. The

God whose holiness fills the earth. The God whose presence knows no bounds. The God whose knowledge knows no end. The God whose being is love—such love that it spills over to create wondrous worlds of intense beauty and beings he might love for eternity. By God's unfathomable grace, we can now share in the very glory that is shared by the Father and the Son. As Jesus puts it, "I have given them the glory you gave me" (John 17:22).

This unity between God and man is not merely the emphasis of the Gospel of John. We find it at the heart of Paul's theology as well. In Colossians 1 he waxes eloquent about the nature of Christ. He says that "Christ is the visible image of the invisible God." Then Paul notes that "God in all his fullness was pleased to live *in Christ*." And that Christ on the cross "made peace with everything in heaven and on earth." Then Paul concludes, "Now he has reconciled you to himself through the death of Christ in his physical body. As a result, he has brought you *into his own presence*" (Colossians 1:15-22, emphasis added).

In the same letter, Paul talks about the message he has been commissioned to proclaim. This message was kept secret in ages past, but no longer. And he says, "This is the secret: Christ lives in you. This gives you assurance of sharing his glory" (Colossians 1:27).

In Ephesians Paul says the same thing in a different context. He's talking about how our sin has led to our death. This is a classic passage about grace and faith. But note the goal of God's work:

*God is so rich in mercy, and he loved us so much, that
even though we were dead because of our sins, he gave
us life when he raised Christ from the dead. (It is only
by God's grace that you have been saved!) For he raised
us from the dead along with Christ and seated us with
him in the heavenly realms because we* are united with
Christ Jesus.

(EPHESIANS 2:4-6, EMPHASIS ADDED)

Peter sums it up quite succinctly when he writes that God
has "called us to himself by means of his marvelous glory and
excellence. And because of his glory and excellence, he has
given us great and precious promises. These are the promises that enable us *to share his divine nature*" (2 Peter 1:3-4,
emphasis added).

When we ponder such love—a love that would draw
us into the very being of God—we are naturally amazed.
We were lost, but now we're found. We were dead, but now
we're alive. We were alienated, but now we're immersed in his
acceptance. And this gives us no small amount of joy.

But we often fail to see that God was not merely being
kind to us in Christ. He wasn't just helping us because we
were in desperate straits. (And we were! There was indeed no
hope for us.) But as Paul notes at the beginning of Ephesians,
God delighted to save us for his own good reasons.

*All praise to God, the Father of our Lord Jesus Christ,
who has blessed us with every spiritual blessing in the*

heavenly realms because we are united with Christ. . . .
God decided in advance to adopt us into his own family
by bringing us to himself through Jesus Christ. This is
what he wanted to do, and it gave him great pleasure.

(EPHESIANS 1:3, 5)

God takes pleasure in living in this intimate, loving fellowship not just with his Son, which he has done for eternity, but with his creatures as well. But because of our sin, which leads to our death, he could not enjoy fellowship with the people he created. We are alienated from him by our sin, dead to him in our trespasses, with no fellowship possible. So he comes to us in Christ to forgive our sins and reconcile us to himself so we might be united with him and have fellowship with him for eternity.

Because he wants to.

Life in God

Through Christ, we are now embedded in the very being of God. What that means precisely would take a library of books to explain. In fact, the history of Christian poetry and preaching and song is replete with attempts to describe our wondrous unity with the Father.

Let's look at two examples. The first comes from Jonathan Edwards, the eighteenth-century American theologian. In his sermon "The Excellency of Christ" he highlights one dimension of the divine nature in which we now participate:

Christ, as he is God, is infinitely great and high
above all. He is higher than the kings of the earth;
for he is King of kings, and Lord of lords. He is
higher than the heavens, and higher than the highest
angels of heaven. . . . Christ is the Creator and
great Possessor of heaven and earth. He is sovereign
Lord of all. He rules over the whole universe, and
doth whatsoever pleased him. His knowledge is
without bound. His wisdom is perfect, and what
none can circumvent. His power is infinite, and
none can resist Him. His riches are immense and
inexhaustible.[11]

Second, the famous British preacher Charles Spurgeon,
in the last sermon he ever preached, talked about the nature
of the royalty we now share in God:

There never was his like among the choicest of
princes. He is always to be found in the thickest part
of the battle. When the wind blows cold he always
takes the bleak side of the hill. The heaviest end of
the cross lies ever on his shoulders. If he bids us carry
a burden, he carries it also. If there is anything that is
gracious, generous, kind, and tender, yea lavish and
superabundant in love, you always find it in him.[12]

Only when we begin to see God as Lover can we grasp
God as Creator and Lord. He may indeed be a Lawgiver, but

now we see clearly that the law is given to show us how to live in love with him and with one another. It's not an arbitrary set of rules for how to be righteous. It is a love manual.

And only when we see God as Lover can we understand how God is more than mere Agent. As wonderful as it is to experience the benefits of his grace and mercy, they should never be the focal point. The minute they become the focus, they disappear. It's like happiness—make it your goal, and you'll never reach it. The blessings of life in Christ, like happiness, are the result of something else, something that has objectively happened—Christ's death and resurrection. And it's something that, through the power of the Holy Spirit, allows us to penetrate the mystery of God himself. As the great hymn "Be Thou My Vision" puts it,

> *Be Thou my Vision, O Lord of my heart;*
> *Naught be all else to me, save that Thou art. . . .*
> *Thou my great Father, and I Thy true son,*
> *Thou in me dwelling, and I with Thee one.*

We cannot neatly separate who God is from what he does for us, for it is the very nature of God to pour out his love to others. But the way we think about his love is crucial if we are to keep the center at the center. Jonathan Edwards says "Divine knowledge and Divine love, go together. . . . When persons have a true discovery of the excellency and sufficiency of Christ," they naturally are filled with love for God and others:

When they experience a right belief of the truth of
the gospel, such a belief is accompanied by love.
They love him whom they believe to be the Christ,
the Son of the living God. . . . When persons
experience a true trust and reliance on Christ, they
rely on him with love, and so do it with delight
and sweet acquiescence of soul. . . . When persons
experience true comfort and spiritual joy, their joy
is the joy of faith and love. They do not rejoice in
themselves, *but it is God who is their exceeding joy.*[13]
(emphasis added)

As great as forgiveness is, it is not our exceeding joy. As
wonderful as are the blessings of salvation, they are not our
exceeding joy. Our exceeding joy is God, the God who has
brought us into his very presence through Jesus Christ. How
exactly he did that, the subject of the next chapter, is nearly
as extraordinary as the fact that he did.

CHAPTER 3

Becoming One Again

WHEN I WAS IN COLLEGE, my girlfriend and I went to the movie *Summer of '42*. I haven't seen the movie in forty years, but here's what I remember: it was a coming-of-age story, it portrayed vividly the friendship of a group of teenage guys, and afterward it made me weep uncontrollably.

My girlfriend didn't know what to do with me because I just kept crying. I didn't know what to do with me either, because I didn't know what was going on. It took me years to figure it out.

I finally realized that the story reminded me of my child-hood, which was the happiest time of my life. I had a group of friends who spent every afternoon and most weekends together. We played baseball in the spring and summer, football in the fall, and "army" in the winter. We rode our bikes to the suburban shopping center to buy baseball cards and then spent hours organizing and trading them. We set up war scenarios in the orchard that bumped up against our suburban tract.

We had fights, of course: I won my first, lost my second, and then retired. We had rivalries: some of us rooted for the Los Angeles Dodgers, although most of us were San Francisco Giants fans. But through it all we remained friends. Unlike the coming-of-age movie, there were no experiments with smoking or drinking or sex. We were just a group of pre-adolescent guys who loved being together.

And then, life intervened. One of my friends betrayed me. Another moved away. We entered junior high school, and we each formed new friendships. Then I moved away and lost touch with everyone. It had never occurred to me how much I loved that time in my life—and how much I missed it—until I found myself sobbing that night in college. I later understood that I grieved the passing of the innocence, the joy, and the love I'd shared with those friends. I hadn't realized how much I yearned to reconnect with that time and how sad I was that I never could.

Maybe for you this idyllic time occurred in high school or college, or maybe in your first years of marriage. But, for whatever reasons, the best time in your life is now gone, and it seems impossible to restore the lost connections with those you so dearly loved. Such experiences are a micro-cosm of our world of broken relationships—relationships that have been torn apart by pride or greed or disease or all of the above. We live in a world of war and rumors of war, of disease and poverty, of slavery and sex trafficking, of addictions and crime, and of everyday, run-of-the-mill selfishness.

All of us have experienced the pain of this world's brokenness in very personal ways. It's part of the human experience. I guarantee that just like me, one day you will find yourself aching—or weeping, as I did—for restoration. Some part of the broken world will touch your life, and you will cry out for wholeness. Maybe you feel that way today. At some point we all feel it deep down in our souls.

The reason I cried that day and the reason all of us ache sometimes is because we know intuitively that this world used to be a better place. We may not recognize this consciously—some even try to deny it. But we are aware that this isn't the way things are supposed to be, that there once was a time when things weren't broken. Christians know this place as Eden, and we know that something happened there that got us where we are today. Broken. Aching. Yearning for something better.

Love Wins clearly recognizes the brokenness of our lives and of our world. And it is deeply concerned with explaining how the brokenness is healed. A lot of what it says illuminates much that is wrong and much that God has done to restore things. But the biblical picture, it turns out, illuminates much more and shows even more deeply what God has done to heal the brokenness.

Seven Deadly Realities

The Bible talks about the human problem in many different ways. For instance, we sin against God, we hurt ourselves and others, we break the laws of God and the laws of the land, we fail to care for the creation around us. For the purposes of this book, though, I'm thinking of the problem in general terms of "deadly realities." Here I've listed several of the deadly realities we face as human beings:

1. *Alienation from God.* This is the immediate result after Adam and Eve eat the forbidden fruit. The first thing God asks is, "Adam, where are you?" This separation signals a dramatic rupture in what had been a close, loving relationship.
2. *Injustice.* The injustice first rears its terrible head with Cain's murder of Abel. Ever since then, evil has been embedded in every human society. From the beginning, the human problem has been both spiritual and social.
3. *Sin and guilt.* When human beings disobey the gracious commands of God, we are objectively guilty. This reality is usually accompanied by an uneasy feeling. Both the objective fact and the feeling are called guilt. At its core, though, sin is not so much breaking an external law as it is rejecting God in one's life.
4. *Slavery.* Sometimes the Bible describes sin as if it were what we'd call an addiction. We simply cannot

stop disobeying the gracious commands of God, and so we cannot find our way back to him. Other times the language is more personal, telling how evil spiritual powers hold us in their grip, enslaving us and preventing us from doing the good and driving us toward our death.

5. *Darkness.* Ultimately, we are blind to the desperate reality of our situation. We get hints of the human tragedy here and there, but we can't even begin to imagine how hopeless our state is. We blind ourselves to our situation by creating religious and philosophical systems, hoping that if we try a little harder, we can remedy our problem ourselves. But our darkness only grows darker.

6. *Death.* The Bible says death is the consequence of sin. This makes sense if we understand sin as the rejection of the living God. If we disconnect ourselves from the source of life, our trajectory can be nothing but death.

7. *Hopelessness.* Since death is our trajectory, and since we are addicted to sin and blind to the reality of our lot, our situation really is hopeless. There is nothing that can be done from our side of things to heal the breach with God that has caused this horrific state of affairs.

As we face these seven deadly realities, we quickly realize we're in a situation that is impossible for us to fix.

Think of a country like Rwanda. The nation breaks out in a horrible spasm of genocide, with half the nation trying to kill the other half and the other half retaliating however it can. After a hundred days it's over—but now 20 percent of the population is dead. Everyone in the country personally knows someone who was cruelly murdered. Everyone personally knows a murderer. So what do you do? Forgive and forget? That would be a scandal to justice. Put every murderer in jail? There are not enough jails in all of Africa to house the murderers, and what court system anywhere could handle the backlog? How do you bring justice to injustice on a scale no one can begin to fathom? Is there any way for human beings to restore Rwanda, to bring healing, to balance the scales of justice and forgiveness?

Or take something more personal. Two parents discover their college-age son is doing drugs. He gets evicted from his apartment and asks to live at home. Of course the parents want to welcome him, but not if the young man is going to continue to do drugs in disobedience of the law and of their wishes for him. But to make him fend for himself on the streets in the drug culture may be sending him to his death. They might say he can live at home as long as he starts going to rehab. But they also know that forced treatment doesn't usually do the trick. Is there any human solution that guarantees this young man will be restored to his right mind?

If we find such common examples to be impossible situations, how much more impossible is it to bridge the divide between God and us? This divide was begun in the Garden of Eden with humankind's refusal of the gracious and life-giving commands of God. When Adam and Eve took a bite of the forbidden fruit, they took a stab at God. "We don't need you," they were saying, in effect.

It is no surprise that one of the first sins after this rupture is a significant relational break: a murder between two brothers. Cain could never bring back Abel after he had slain him. He was gone forever. In much the same way, humankind's unity with God had been lost forever. As that family murder shows, the fractured relationship between man and God in the Garden unleashed the forces of brokenness throughout the world and for all history. And so we find ourselves deeply grieving what has been forfeited and at a loss as to how to even begin to heal it all.

What we need is a miracle. It can't just be the execution of justice, for then who of us would remain alive? It can't be a sentimental glossing over of our wrongs, as if a simple waving of the hand or a wink of the eye could make the gravity and consequences of sin vanish. We need a forgiveness that punishes injustice, a justice that forgives. That's what it would take to truly restore us to our right minds and to one another. But that combination of realities is impossible. Who could pull it off? It would take a miracle.

The Bible says that the miracle has indeed happened, and it has been accomplished by the very one whom we humans have wished dead—the very being whose beloved creation has been destroyed by our beastly behavior. The miracle is called atonement: "at-one-ment." Putting something that is split in two back into one. Bringing two alienated parties back together in harmony. Restoring, healing, reconciling the whole world.

The Bible teaches that the atonement that "fits the crime" of sin is accomplished by one who is free from sin. On the cross, one who has known perfect fellowship from eternity endures the brokenness we all deserve; the Author of life experiences the death we all have coming. In this way, injustice is accounted for, taken with the seriousness that it demands. In this way, forgiveness that is not mere sentimentalism is offered. In this way, the two become one, God with man, man with man, all over the universe. That's atonement.

How can this be? It doesn't make logical sense. How does the death of an innocent man make things right with those who are guilty before God? How does the death of an innocent God count as anything but a tragedy? But that's the key: we're not dealing with logic alone here. This is not a truth we could infer by looking at the way the world works. We're talking about something that has been revealed as true by God himself.

But it is a truth that we get hints of from time to time, isn't it?

We get a hint of atonement in our sense that injustice must be paid for. That was the predominant reaction of Americans when the death of Osama bin Laden was announced. He was the man behind the murder of three thousand on 9/11, the one who inspired acts of terrorism that killed hundreds more. His death did not really fit the crime, though, did it? One man's death did not make up for the death and suffering that he had caused thousands. Even though many, on hearing the news, said, "Justice was done," it really wasn't done fully, was it? Still, this sense that injustice must be paid for arose in our hearts.

We also get a hint of atonement in our sense that an innocent death may redeem. Martin Luther King Jr. was a prophet among us who reminded all, and especially Americans, of our sin of racism. When he was killed, there was a feeling in America that, while he was certainly killed *because* of it, he had also in a way died *for* our sin of racism. Although King's death could never really atone for our centuries of racism, his death revealed our racism as real and heinous; it prompted us to not only confess that sin but also begin to change.

In his death, Jesus Christ judged sin for what it is so that no one else would *have to* endure the just consequences of our sin. Jesus' innocent death made possible our reconciliation— a reconciliation grounded in expensive grace, grace that takes sin seriously. The Cross is not something that merely reminds us of our sin and moves us to better behavior; it actually crushes sin and fills those who respond in faith with new life. In short, Jesus died for us so that we might live in him.

The Bible talks about it this way:

When we were utterly helpless, Christ came at just the right time and died for us sinners.

(ROMANS 5:6)

Because God's children are human beings—made of flesh and blood—the Son also became flesh and blood.

*For only as a human being could he die, and only by
dying could he break the power of the devil, who had
the power of death. Only in this way could he set free all
who have lived their lives as slaves to the fear of dying.*
(HEBREWS 2:14-15)

*Adam's one sin brings condemnation for everyone,
but Christ's one act of righteousness brings a right
relationship with God and new life for everyone.*
(ROMANS 5:18)

*God was in Christ, reconciling the world to himself, no
longer counting people's sins against them. And he gave us
this wonderful message of reconciliation. So we are Christ's
ambassadors; God is making his appeal through us. We
speak for Christ when we plead, "Come back to God!"*
(2 CORINTHIANS 5:19-20)

That's the unbelievable story of the Bible.

That's the impossible possibility of the church's proclamation.

That's the Good News.

Deeper than a Personal Relationship

It's crucial to note here that, according to the Bible, the whole
point is life in and with God, no matter which atonement
metaphor is used. The story begins and ends with our union
with God. Between those two ends, though, is the breaking

of that relationship and the forging of a more profound one—a process better called "abundant life," or participation in the life of God. What does this participation look like? There are many ways we can picture it.

To live in God is like a child living in the womb of his or her mother, literally *in* her, drawing life and nourishment from her.

To live in God is like thriving in a great marriage, in which through the years, husband and wife become one in heart, mind, and soul. It is not an accident that in the most intimate act of marriage, man and woman, in a sense, merge and live in each other.

To live in God is like a branch being connected to a vine, drawing its sustenance from the vine.

Allowing God to live in us is like breathing in life-giving air, without which we would quickly die.

Allowing God to live in us is like drinking living water so that we will never thirst again.

All these analogies, which come from Scripture,[14] help us grasp what is still ultimately a mystery: Jesus in the Father and in us. We in Jesus and in the Father. Participation in the very life of the Trinity. Not a mystical absorption into the divine, but a relationship so personal, so intimate, so close that Jesus says we're one with God yet still in a relationship between parties.

But not just two parties. To grasp more completely this amazing life, we need to introduce two others.

First, all the disciples—that is, the church, the fellowship of all believers in Jesus Christ. It's not just that the disciples *as individuals* participate in the life of God. No, Jesus is clear that he wants them to *be one* as he and his Father are one. He wants them, too, to share a unified life, enjoying unity of will, of desire, and of purpose. So as the disciples participate in unity among themselves, they also participate in the unity of Father, Son, and Holy Spirit.

Second, the Holy Spirit, the glue that holds this whole thing together. The Holy Spirit is the divine person who connects us to Jesus and the Father and to one another. We cannot understand what salvation is, what it means to love and be loved by God, until we know, as Paul says, "how dearly God loves us, because he has given us the Holy Spirit to fill our hearts with his love" (Romans 5:5).

In light of all this, we can now see how Christ, in one fell swoop, deals with every problem—each "deadly reality"—that plagues humankind.

- Because of the Cross and the Resurrection, God forgives our sins and reconciles us to himself (2 Corinthians 5:19; Colossians 1:21-22).
- Once we respond in faith to what Christ has done, we "come back to God" (2 Corinthians 5:20) and are "made right with him" (Galatians 2:17).
- Now we are intimately reconnected with God; we live in his love. Living in true love, our estrangement with others is overcome (Ephesians 2:16).
- Since we are in relationship with the light of God himself, we no longer walk in darkness (John 8:12).

- Since our fellowship is with a righteous and just God, we know that righteousness and justice will eventually prevail among those who participate in the life of God (Psalm 89:14-15).
- Since we are now part and parcel of God's *life*, we can no more die than he can (John 5:24).
- Since all this is true, our situation is far from hopeless. Instead, our hope overflows (Hebrews 6:19).

He puts us and the whole universe back together again, and together with him.

Sacrificing Sacrifice

Three people walk out of an Academy Award–winning movie, each thinking the movie was great . . . but each for different reasons. One was viscerally moved by the beautiful cinematography, one was convinced that the acting made it captivating and believable, and one insisted that it would all be nothing without the strong screenplay. If you talked to only one of the viewers, you might get a partial review of the movie's strengths, but it's only after you hear each report that the full depth of the picture really emerges.

It's like that with the atonement. The Holy Spirit gave different biblical insights into what exactly happened on the Cross, each one illuminating some crucial aspect of the atonement. *Love Wins* does a good job of reminding readers about this. As the book puts it,

What happened on the cross is like . . .

a defendant going free,

a relationship being reconciled,

something lost being redeemed,

a battle being won,

a final sacrifice being offered,

so that no one ever has to offer another one again,

an enemy being loved.[15]

The book does note that different metaphors highlight different aspects of salvation. But it concludes, "The point, then, isn't to narrow it to one particular metaphor. . . .The point then, as it is now, is Jesus. The divine in flesh and blood. He's where the life is."[16]

Well, yes and no. Yes, the point is Jesus. But it's not merely Jesus "the divine in flesh and blood." To limit Jesus to that description is to suggest that it is the Incarnation alone that saves us, that the Cross and the Resurrection are secondary. I don't believe this limited view is intentional, but given how *Love Wins* talks about the Cross and the Resurrection throughout the book, it starts to seem that way.

In fact, the book has little positive to say about one atonement theory—the sacrifice theory, or what is sometimes referred to as substitutionary atonement. *Love Wins* says that sacrifice may have been a meaningful way to talk about Christ's death in biblical times, and today in "primitive cultures around the world that do continue to understand sin, guilt, and atonement in those ways"[17]—the unfortunate suggestion being that people who believe in sin, guilt, and atonement in terms of sacrifice are "primitive."

Further, *Love Wins* notes "the brilliant, creative work these first Christians were doing when they used these images and metaphors."[18] This suggests that these ideas were of human origin and not divine revelation. And that we no longer have to use them if they are not meaningful to contemporary culture. The implication is clear when it comes to substitutionary atonement: it's artificial, irrelevant, and disposable.

This is an especially confusing point given that large portions of the books Romans, Galatians, and Hebrews, among other parts of the Bible, are devoted to helping readers understand substitutionary atonement.[19]

Victory over Guilt, Too

Love Wins implicitly favors two other theories of the atonement, the first of which has been called *Christus Victor*. This theory emphasizes Christ's freeing us from our slavery to sin, winning for us a victory against all the evil powers that enslave the universe. As the book accurately notes, atonement is much more than merely having a personal relationship with God:

For the first Christians, the story was, first and foremost, bigger, grander. More massive. . . . God

has inaugurated a movement in Jesus' resurrection
to renew, restore, and reconcile everything "on earth
or in heaven," just as God originally intended it.
The powers of death and destruction have been
defeated on the most epic scale imaginable.[20]

This description of the atonement parallels the biblical picture of salvation that we will discuss in this book, too. Though we'll address some crucial differences in later chapters (for example, in *Love Wins*, reconciliation with God ends up being a secondary rather than a primary theme), I for one applaud the emphasis that the biblical model of Christus Victor offers: salvation is not just about "me and Jesus," but about the future of the universe. It's not just about personal forgiveness of sins, but about the victory of Christ over the powers of evil.

In *Love Wins*, however, Christus Victor ends up being taught *at the expense of* sacrifice. Substitutionary atonement is marginalized, pictured as outdated and meaningful only for "primitive" people. This is a serious distortion of the full biblical picture, and thus it dilutes the Good News.

Yes, we are enslaved to spiritual powers, both personally and corporately. But the Bible's teaching on Christ's sacrifice for our sins is crucial because it deals with a rather crucial human problem: human guilt for the state of the world. It's not that evil powers have mysteriously taken control of everything, including our lives, all on their own. It is our sin, our disobedience to the gracious commands of God, that ushers in a world of evil and death.

G. K. Chesterton was once asked to describe what he thought was the core problem of the world. He famously replied, "I am."

Now, this much *Love Wins* does acknowledge, noting "our role in corrupting this world."[21] But in Scripture, the main problem with our sin is not that it messes up the world. It's not so much an offense against the world but against God. As the psalmist puts it, "Against you, and you alone, have I sinned; I have done what is evil in your sight" (Psalm 51:4). This aspect of sin is, as far as I could tell, not accounted for in the book.

To take myself as an example, *I* am the problem, not some evil force out there. The main problem is between me and God; yes, I am also victim to spiritual forces, but I'm the one who often invites those forces into my life in the first place. Not only do I need to be freed from this problem, but I also—and especially—need to be forgiven of it.

So we need both models of atonement. We need to acknowledge both realities, in their full horror and dread. But when it comes to sin and evil, *Love Wins* nearly always emphasizes our being affected by it, not our responsibility for it. As a consequence, it cannot adequately describe the fullness of the salvation offered to us in Christ.

It's Not Just about Us

The other atonement idea endorsed by *Love Wins* is what theologians call the moral theory of atonement. The idea is this: if you understand Christ's death on the cross as an act of supreme love, that will prompt you to live in love for others. It's like being inspired to volunteer to tutor because a friend we admire is doing it. We are saved from selfishness by pondering the unselfishness of Christ on the cross. Here's an example from *Love Wins*:

> When we say yes to God, when we open ourselves to Jesus's living, giving act on the cross, we enter into a way of life. He is the source, the strength, the example, and the assurance that this pattern of death and rebirth is the way into the only kind of life that actually sustains and inspires.[22]

Another passage says that "the cross continues to endure" because "it's a reminder, a sign, a glimpse, an icon that allows us to tap into our deepest longings to be part of a new creation."[23]

Yes, Christ's self-giving inspires us to live for others. And, yes, our deepest longings are indeed satisfied in Christ. Thank God! But one cannot help but notice how relentlessly human centered these descriptions are. The Cross becomes about our getting inspired and being sustained. Salvation becomes about something that satisfies our deepest longings.

The New Testament, on the other hand, has very little to say about our emotional reactions to the Cross. It's much more interested in what objectively transpired there. Among other things, before Christ's death on the cross, we were "dead" in our sins, "obeying the devil." Christ's death and resurrection "gave us life" and "raised us from the dead"

(Ephesians 2:1-7). But the Cross reconciles us to God and brings us into such an intimate connection with him that Paul can go so far as to say, "It is no longer I who live, but Christ lives in me" (Galatians 2:20).

When this gift is received in faith, it's not just that our feelings get changed; we become one with Christ, who is one with the Father—and who is now one with us. We share in God's life, together with the whole body of believers. It's not primarily about the love we experience and practice in our lives but also about the connection with God and with one another, participating together in God's very life and being.

It's not just about what we experience but about what God has done.

More than a Rite of Spring

There is one more atonement misunderstanding in *Love Wins* that should be cleared up, and it's a misunderstanding shared by many Christians. It has to do with the death and resurrection of Jesus Christ.

Many Christians imagine that Christ's death and resurrection are just like the cycles of birth and death we see in nature. Trees lose their leaves in the fall and grow new ones in the spring. Crops die in the fall and then come alive in the spring. *Love Wins* plays up this idea, apparently trying to help readers see how natural it is to believe in Jesus' death and resurrection as something that makes perfect sense. The book represents the Cross as "a symbol of an elemental reality, one we all experience," and the Resurrection not as a new concept but as "something that has always been true." It's portrayed as another instance of "this pattern of death and rebirth" and "how the universe works."[24]

But if resurrection is a universal pattern we see day in and day out, why did Jesus need to go to the trouble of dying a cruel death on a cross? If this is how the world already works, why all the bother? Couldn't people just believe that, without Jesus having to die and be raised again? Don't most people already believe in this pattern of death and rebirth?

Yes, they do. Because, in fact, religion that focuses on the *universal* sequence of life, death, and rebirth is a very old one. The ancient world was awash in nature mysticism and fertility cults that taught the eternal pattern of death and new life. These were religions that determined their ethics and rituals by observing the natural cycle of rebirth. But this is not biblical religion. The Cross is not the universal symbol of death and resurrection, the general truth of which we can see in plant life and seasonal cycles. No, it is a judgment against human sin, of which we are all individually guilty. It is also an act of grace, which none of us deserves.

Furthermore, according to the Bible, the resurrection of Jesus is not the universal symbol of new life. It is, rather, the vindication of Christ's work on the cross. It proves Jesus was right. In the earliest sermons, the apostles used the Resurrection to tell their listeners, "The man you crucified . . . God raised from the dead. . . . There is salvation in no one else!" (Acts 4:10-12).

That's why the doctrine of the Cross and the Resurrection is not always a comforting one or one with which everyone is already familiar. No, it is still a scandal and a stumbling block for many. It shows us our sin, our absolute dependence on God for forgiveness and new life. This is good news for many people. But it is disturbing news for those who depend on their own efforts for salvation.

So desperate are we, and so desperate, it seems, is *Love Wins*, that we're tempted to take the edge off the Cross and the Resurrection, to soften the blow of the miracle, to make them icons and metaphors of truths we already know rather than convicting and liberating—if shocking—realities.

John Updike's poem "Seven Stanzas at Easter" makes a statement about the Resurrection that applies to all the central teachings of the New Testament:

> *Let us not mock God with metaphor,*
> *analogy, sidestepping, transcendence;*
> *making of the event a parable, a sign painted in the*
> *faded credulity of earlier ages:*
> *let us walk through the door.*

In fact, the Resurrection is precisely the opposite of the way the universe works. In the universe as we know it, we die. That's it. That's the end of the story. Nothing in the universe suggests that after we die we will rise again. Nothing—until Jesus rises again.

The Cross and the Resurrection do not show how the universe works; they show how God works. This is not something we already know but something so extraordinary it has to be revealed to us by the Holy Spirit.

Let me be clear. I don't think any Christian who compares the Cross and the Resurrection to the natural life cycle is a pagan. Hardly. Most of those who do it are well meaning. But we need to see how unbiblical this view is at its core. And how it inadvertently sabotages the goodness of the Good News. It turns the absolute miracle of the Cross and the Resurrection into old news instead of showing us the miracle that atonement is.

Justice Also Wins

All in all, *Love Wins* ends up talking about the atonement in ways that are remarkably reminiscent of nineteenth-century liberalism. In many parts, it feels like a discussion about "a God without wrath [who] brought men without sin into a kingdom without judgment through the ministrations of a Christ without a cross."[25] This is H. Richard Niebuhr's classic summary of theological liberalism.

The parallels are not exact, for they never are. In fact, *Love Wins* is boldly orthodox on a number of doctrines that nineteenth-century liberalism denied: the deity of Christ and the bodily Resurrection, to name just two. Certainly, to say that a book uses arguments favored by liberals does not make it a liberal book. It mainly suggests that in using such arguments, the book is probably talking about the truly *Good* News.

I do not believe *Love Wins* reflects the thickness of biblical revelation nor of lived reality. Most of the atonement it articulates is true as far as it goes. Because this view discards the idea of sacrifice and substitutionary atonement, though, it cannot go far enough or deep enough, and thus it cannot go high enough. The book is so anxious to show that love wins, it fails to appreciate how important it is that justice also wins.

As Paul notes, in the sacrifice of Christ Jesus not only are we "made right with God" through faith—by grace—but this was also done "to demonstrate his righteousness, for he himself is fair and just, and he declares sinners to be right in his sight when they believe in Jesus" (Romans 3:25-26). Jonathan Edwards puts it this way:

> There meet in Jesus Christ, infinite justice, and infinite grace. As Christ is a divine person he is infinitely holy and just, infinitely hating sin, and disposed to execute condign punishment for sin. He is the Judge of the world, and the infinitely just judge of it, and will not acquit at all the wicked, or by any means clear the guilty.
>
> And yet he is one that is infinitely gracious and merciful. Though his justice be so strict with respect to all sin, and every breach of the law, yet he has

grace sufficient for every sinner, and even the chief of sinners. And it is not only sufficient for the most unworthy to show them mercy, and bestow some good upon them, but to bestow the greatest good.[26]

What is broken will be made whole again. What was lost in Eden will be regained. Love wins. Justice wins. And the God who is perfectly just and perfectly merciful wins.

CHAPTER 4

The Wonder of Faith

HOW EXACTLY do we come to share in the life of God? How do we become one with Jesus, who is one with the Father and who is then one with us? In a word, faith.

But faith is a deep mystery of the Christian life, and something that is easy to get confused about. In fact, the view of faith assumed in *Love Wins* is one of the biggest stumbling blocks in the book. Unfortunately, its view on this matter is not uncommon in the church today.

In order for us to more fully appreciate faith, it's a good idea to look at what faith is like in the New Testament. We begin with an incident that occurred right after the resurrection of Jesus.

Recognizing Jesus

After the death of Jesus, two of his disciples were walking to
a village named Emmaus, about seven miles from Jerusalem,
and talking about the stunning turn of events that had just
happened. At the beginning of the previous week, Jesus had
entered Jerusalem in triumph, with crowds treating him like
the Messiah. By midweek, they were shouting for his crucifixion. By week's end, Jesus was dead. It must have left the
disciples bewildered. As they talked, suddenly their master,
Jesus, came up beside them and started walking with them.
He asked, "What are you discussing so intently?"

One of them, Cleopas, replied, "You must be the only
person in Jerusalem who hasn't heard about all the things
that have happened there the last few days."

"What things?" Jesus asked. So the two started to tell
Jesus about what had happened.

This is strange, isn't it? These disciples clearly do not
know who they are talking to! They do not recognize who
Jesus is. How do we explain this?

Some interpreters speculate that the disciples' hearts were
so filled with grief and their eyes so clouded with tears that
they simply couldn't see straight. Others say that Jesus' resurrection body had been transformed, so much so that the
disciples couldn't recognize him. Luke, the author of this
Gospel, gets right to the point: "God kept them from recognizing him" (Luke 24:16).

Not their grief. Not his new body. God simply did not

let them perceive that their Savior was talking with them. As the conversation wore on, Jesus ended up explaining how, if they would remember their Scriptures, it all made sense: the Messiah would have to suffer and die before he entered into glory. Then Jesus gave them a long lesson "explaining from all the Scriptures the things concerning himself" (Luke 24:27).

By this time, evening was upon them. As they approached Emmaus, the two disciples asked Jesus to stay the night and share a meal with them. That's when it happened.

As they sat down to eat, Jesus "took the bread and blessed it," Luke writes. "Then he broke it and gave it to them. Suddenly, their eyes were opened, and they recognized him" (Luke 24:30-31). And though Luke doesn't actually say this next part, he doesn't have to, given how he has set up the story: their eyes are opened *by God*. Only because of God's power do they recognize Jesus.

Many Christians can identify with this conversion story. C. S. Lewis describes his conversion from atheism to theism (but not yet to Christianity) in a similar way. As he began a bus ride one afternoon, he was an atheist; he did not believe in God. By the time he reached his destination, Lewis says in *Surprised by Joy*, he had "unbuckled [his] armor," which led to a prayer from his knees some nights later.[27] He does not say this "unbuckling" was characterized by either thought or emotion. He doesn't say he had a vision. The way he describes it, it was not so much a rational decision—consummate rational thinker though he was—as a recognition of reality.

In Luke's language, God opened Lewis's eyes so that he could recognize God.

That's one way that faith comes to people. But there are other ways too.

Overwhelming Love

The next story also takes place on a road. On this road traveled Saul of Tarsus, the Jewish leader who was furious with early Christians for subverting Judaism. As the story begins, he is on his way from Jerusalem to Damascus to find Christians, arrest them, and drag them back to Jerusalem in chains for trial and punishment.

As Saul walks along, Luke (who relates this story also) says, "A light from heaven suddenly shone down around him." Saul was knocked to the ground; then a voice thundered out, "Saul! Saul! Why are you persecuting me?"

Saul replied, "Who are you, lord?"

"I am Jesus, the one you are persecuting!" (Acts 9:1-5).

Jesus, a mysterious stranger to the two disciples on the road to Emmaus, made himself known to Saul plainly, dramatically, and in a way that frightened him. Jesus told him to go into Damascus and wait there for further instructions. When Saul stood up and opened his eyes, he found he was blind.

Bright light, thrown off balance, blinded—do you think Jesus got Saul's attention? If that first encounter didn't do the trick, the next one did. Three days later Saul's sight was restored by the prayers of a Christian named Ananias. Should we be surprised that Saul (now known as the apostle Paul) started following Jesus? A better question might be, did he really have any choice in the matter? Who wouldn't believe after such an encounter?

We've all heard similar stories in our day. One was told in my church recently. An elderly woman, Silvia, was pushed in her wheelchair onto the stage during worship so she could tell her story. She talked about how she had ignored God her whole life, how she had never even shown any interest in Jesus, and how just one year earlier that had all changed. Her health had started to rapidly decline. As her condition worsened, she slowly became bitter and despondent. She said she just wanted to die.

One of the nurses who was helping her was a Christian, and she encouraged Silvia to read her Bible, pray, and trust in Christ. Silvia made halting efforts, but to no avail. She confessed to her nurse that she didn't even know how to pray or what to pray. So the nurse taught her the Lord's Prayer and told her to say it whenever she was discouraged.

One day while Silvia sat despondently in a waiting room before yet another doctor's appointment, she began reciting the Lord's Prayer. Suddenly, she says, the room was filled with light and an overwhelming sense of peace. Immediately she knew that it was the Holy Spirit and that he was telling her God loved her and everything was going to be all right. And that's when her life turned a corner. Her bitterness departed; her despair turned to joy. Even her health began to improve, though she still suffers from many illnesses. She is at the far end of a long life, probably without more than a few years left to live. But as she said in her testimony, she now lives with a peace and joy she had never known before.

Did Silvia decide, of her own free will, to give her life to Jesus? Or did Jesus, in his good will, miraculously give to her, as he did to Saul of Tarsus, new life?

Wonderful but Not Simple

We assume that faith is simply a matter of choice: we can choose to believe in Jesus or not to believe in Jesus. It's something we can just decide on anytime we like. According to the Bible, though, it's not that simple. Sometimes the reality of Jesus is hidden from people for a time, and then at times the presence of Christ literally overwhelms people and they can hardly *not* believe. But whatever the circumstances, what the Bible plainly teaches is that we come to faith only by the gracious intervention of God.

In one of his teaching sessions, Jesus says this:

> *I am the bread of life. Whoever comes to me will never be hungry again. Whoever believes in me will never be thirsty. But you haven't believed in me even though you have seen me. However, those the Father has given me will come to me, and I will never reject them. . . . And this is the will of God, that I should not lose even one of all those he has given me, but that I should raise them up at the last day.*
>
> (JOHN 6:35-37, 39)

A bit later he reinforces the point: "No one can come to me unless the Father . . . draws them to me, and at the last day I will raise them up" (John 6:44). There's that sense of direct involvement again: according to Jesus, people can't believe in him unless the Father draws them.

Furthermore and more difficult to understand is what is noted here within the Gospel of John—that sometimes God actually makes it impossible for people to believe:

Despite all the miraculous signs Jesus had done, most of the people still did not believe in him. This is exactly what Isaiah the prophet had predicted:

"LORD, who has believed our message?
To whom has the LORD revealed his powerful arm?"

But the people couldn't believe, for as Isaiah also said,

"The Lord has blinded their eyes
and hardened their hearts—
so that their eyes cannot see,
and their hearts cannot understand,
and they cannot turn to me
and have me heal them."

(JOHN 12:37-40)

Some interpret this passage to mean that God hardened their hearts because they refused to believe. But the passage clearly states that they couldn't believe because God had prevented them from believing. It's the type of thing we saw in the story of the two disciples on the road to Emmaus: "God kept them from recognizing him" (Luke 24:16).

This raises more questions than we can tackle in one book, let alone one chapter. But let's look at the biggest objection: that the Lord hardens some hearts. When we read that, we react in shock. We feel like protesting, "That's so arbitrary! That's completely unfair!" And the answer to that protest is not always an immediately satisfying one, because this is a hard issue for us to understand.

The answer is that if God were like us—weak, blind, fickle, ignorant, mercurial, prideful—his actions would indeed be arbitrary and unfair, incredibly and tragically so. But the God we are dealing with—the one Jesus reveals to us—is a God who has shown himself to be perfectly just and perfectly merciful. He's the God who both punished sin and offered forgiveness when, in the person of Christ, he went to the cross. The answer, as strange as it is simple, is that we can trust him. We can trust him to decide wisely and fairly about when and how to reveal himself to us.

Our only other choice is to leave faith in the hands of those who have, time and again, proven themselves anything but just and merciful and wise, who are known to be shortsighted, selfish, and sinful—that is, people like us. That's really not much of a choice.

Some Very Bad News

This is precisely the problem with *Love Wins* and with any belief system that ultimately says that faith is left completely in the hands of sinful and fickle people. That is not good news.

Unfortunately, this is a core principle in *Love Wins*. The chapter "Does God Get What God Wants?" discusses two biblical truths: (1) God is all powerful; he is capable of accomplishing anything he wills, and (2) God desires the salvation of every single person who has ever lived. So, as the chapter's question puts it, does God get what he wants? Won't he use his power to make sure everyone comes to faith in Christ? This is the place where *Love Wins* speculates about whether everyone will eventually be saved. This is a significant question, and there will be more on it in chapter 7 of this book. But toward the end of that chapter in *Love Wins*, the question is set aside because, admittedly, it can't really be answered. Instead,

> There's a better question, one we can answer, one
> that takes all of this speculation about the future . . .
> and brings it back to one absolute we can depend
> on in the midst of all of this, which turns out to be
> another question. It's not "Does God get what God
> wants?" but "Do we get what we want?"[28]

Let's take a moment to note what is being asserted here. The answer to this new question—Do we get what we want?—is, according to the book, the "one absolute we can depend on."

> And the answer to that is a resounding, affirming,
> sure, and positive yes. Yes, we get what we want.
> God is that loving.[29]

What *Love Wins* then argues is that "if we want isolation, despair, and the right to be our own god, God graciously grants us that option." The question we have to ask centers on that word *graciously*. Is that grace? *Love Wins* goes on, "If we insist on using our God-given power and strength to make the world in our own image, God allows us that freedom." Again we have to ask: is that freedom?[30]

"If, however," *Love Wins* claims, "we crave light, we're drawn to truth, we're desperate for grace, . . . God gives us what we want."[31] And so on. The idea is clear. And that idea assumes that we're in charge of our destiny, responsible for our salvation and damnation. Because we get what we want. In fact, this is the "one absolute we can depend on." According to *Love Wins*, this one absolute is also an amazing demonstration of God's love. God shows his great love for us by giving us what we want.

The problem, though, is that this all turns out to be bad news. And sadly it's bad news that has found its way into many churches today.

The attraction to such a view is understandable. In this culture, we don't like to think of God as a judge, and the solution proposed in *Love Wins* would absolve God of that unhappy responsibility. In this interpretation, God doesn't judge people; they judge themselves. Add to that how much we like the idea that we're in charge of our destiny, that we are captains of our fate. We free-spirited Westerners don't like the idea that anyone else, even God, might control our future. But there are many problems with this idea that God gives us what we want.

For example, note what types of character traits this idea is bound to produce. If we are in charge of our destiny, if we are the ones who get salvation because we want it and choose it, then it will be nearly impossible not to become proud and self-righteous. The only difference between us and those who don't know the peace of God is that we've chosen this life and they have not.

That leads to the second temptation that will be nearly impossible to resist: judgmentalism. If those who live in despair do so because that is what they want, because that is what they've chosen, then we can never really have compassion on them. It's their own fault that they live in despair. That's what they wanted; they have to sleep in the bed they've made.

But there is an even deeper problem with this view.

Biblical Problems

According to Scripture, the "one absolute we can depend on" is not the knowledge of what we want, as *Love Wins* asserts. The one absolute we can depend on is the truth that Christ died for our sins and was raised for our salvation. This one absolute is not something about our internal desires; it's about who God has revealed himself to be in Jesus Christ.

In fact, knowing what we want is just about the most uncertain thing in life. At some point in our lives we've all said it: "I'm not sure what I want." And the more important the decision, the more confused most of us become.

I was talking to a friend about his girlfriend. They had been dating for some years and seemed pretty serious. So I asked him if he was going to propose to her. Thus ensued a long conversation in which he told me about the pluses and minuses of getting married, his girlfriend's strengths and weaknesses, his own strengths and weaknesses, and so on and so forth. He didn't know what to do because he really didn't know what he wanted. Did he want to stay single or get married? Did he want this woman, or was there another he would eventually want more?

This may not be everyone's premarital story, but it is typical of human behavior, whether we're talking about small or large decisions. Even when we think we know what we want, we cannot tell what we *really* want. Some people say they don't want to believe in God, but are they really sure?

And when we say, "I want to know God better," we cannot tell what we really want. Do we want to know God, or do we just want to stop feeling guilty for living godless lives? Do we want to know God, or do we just want him to do something in our lives—that is, are we using God for our own agenda? Do we want God, or do we just want to please someone else, like a parent or a spouse who is a devout believer? Our wants are fickle and mysterious. God is mysterious too, but he is not fickle—he is the only one on whom we can absolutely depend. We certainly cannot depend on knowing what we want.

And then there is this: the gospel is not that God loves us so much that he gives us what we want—no, indeed.

The gospel is that God loves us so much that while we were sinners Christ died for us (see Romans 5:8). The gospel is not that God loves us so much that he gives us freedom to choose; it is that God loves us so much that he draws us to believe in him (see John 6:44).

It is not God's *grace* that allows us to be our own gods and thus to suffer isolation and despair. That is the work of God's *judgment*. And it is not that God allows us the freedom to "make the world in our own image." That is not freedom, according to the Bible, but slavery. Slavery to self. Slavery to sin. Slavery to the elemental spirits.

What is assumed in this entire discussion in *Love Wins* is that the human will is free, autonomous, and able to choose between alternatives. The discussion assumes that the will is not fallen, that it needs no salvation, that it doesn't even need help. It assumes that human beings are unbiased moral agents who stand above the fray and make independent decisions about the most important matters.

This is not the biblical picture of humankind but the Enlightenment picture, which turns out to be a fantasy. This view depicts humankind as having unlimited potential and the ability to shape their ultimate destiny. The biblical picture of humankind is radically different—and utterly realistic. People are sinners who find it impossible to choose good consistently, faithfully. They are addicted to the fickle desires of their wicked hearts, so that they simply cannot choose what they want, for it changes all the time, and in the end, they have no idea what they really want.

There has never been a better description of this reality than Paul's:

> *I don't really understand myself, for I want to do what*
> *is right, but I don't do it. Instead, I do what I hate. . . .*
> *And I know that nothing good lives in me, that is, in*
> *my sinful nature. I want to do what is right, but I can't.*
> *I want to do what is good, but I don't. I don't want to*
> *do what is wrong, but I do it anyway.*
>
> (ROMANS 7:15, 18-19)

Humankind, in other words, is anything but free. Instead, we are trapped *by* our sin and trapped *in* our sin. We cannot even see the truth of God. As Paul argues, our minds "are full of darkness," and we "wander far from the life God gives" because we have closed our minds and hardened our hearts against him (Ephesians 4:18). We are not merely lost, but dead in our trespasses (see Colossians 2:13).

In short, the human condition is not full of potential, and it's not simply up to us to choose the right path. No, without the intervention of God, we have about as much hope as a corpse.

And that's the gospel. Not that we have an innate free will, but that God in his freedom came to us to rescue us from spiritual slavery. Through the work of Jesus on the cross, and through the miraculous work of the Holy Spirit, our wills are liberated. Then and only then can we actually recognize Christ, his love, his forgiveness, his grace. Then and only then can we finally respond in faith.

The Role of Response

This can be a pretty hard teaching for American Christians to swallow. We live in a democracy, in which we have the right to vote about our destiny. We live in an economy that exalts choice, and we consumers demand that we have multiple options. Surely religion must work this way too, right? To hear that we cannot even recognize the love of God, let alone respond to it, without the Holy Spirit doing a work in our lives—well, it doesn't always sit well.

At this point let me be clear. I'm not saying that we are mere robots, that we are not called to actually respond to the gospel. But some have gotten in the bad theological habit of putting so much emphasis on the nature of our response that they, like *Love Wins*, make our human will the main thing, letting God's work in Christ drift to the background.

We need to put our response of faith in its proper context. Here's a story to help us do that.

A man finds himself in the middle of a vast sea, treading water. There is no land in sight, no boat on the horizon. He is hungry and thirsty and rapidly tiring. He's headed for death. This man may have free will to swim in one direction or another. He may choose to swim or to tread water. But when it comes to the most important thing, he has no choice—he cannot choose to survive. He's going to drown.

Then along comes a rescue ship. When the ship gets close, it lets out a raft with three men on board. Rowing over to the desperate man, they stretch their arms out over the edge of the raft and grab him. He grabs their arms as they pull him into the boat. They take him on board the ship, give him medical attention, and get him home. The man is saved.

When this man then recounts his story to his family, how will he describe it? Will he say, "Well, the rescuers loved me so much, they pretty much let me decide my fate. And, really, it was my free will that made all the difference." No, he will describe how utterly hopeless his situation was, how grateful he was to see the rescue ship, how wonderful those three men who pulled him aboard were, how excellent the navigator was to find him, and so on.

In this example, the man did, in fact, grab the arms of the rescuers as they reached out to him; he responded. But the truly important thing was not that he responded but that so much had been done by so many to rescue him.

According to Scripture, faith is grabbing on desperately to Christ, who has come to save us (see Hebrews 4:14; 10:23; 1 Peter 1:21). And though it is a free response, the response really is conditional on the rescue. We wouldn't even have the freedom to grab hold of Christ if he hadn't made himself known to us. Salvation is, from first to last, a gift.

But What About . . . ?

I won't pretend that the biblical picture of the enslaved will and the need for God's Spirit does not prompt many questions. Sometimes even the best biblical answers leave a lot unanswered. In this case we naturally wonder, *Why does God ever withhold himself from anyone, even if just for a time? Does he do this forever with some people? Why does he reveal himself so dramatically and undeniably to some people and so quietly and subtly to others? Does he in fact reveal himself to every single person before death?* And so on.

To adhere to the biblical view of salvation by faith does not mean that all our questions are answered, that our theology is all wrapped up and tied with a neat bow. God withholds from us many truths we'd love to know. But that is not to say that we are left completely in the dark.

Among other things, he has clearly revealed this much:

- In the Bible, God paints the most realistic picture of the human situation: we are utterly blind and dead in our natural state.
- God loves us so much that he forgives us and reconciles us to himself in Jesus Christ.
- Through the Holy Spirit, God makes this Good News known to people and unshackles their wills so that, finally, they may grab hold of him.
- Our job is not to delve into the mind of God, or of others, to see how or why or when he works in their innermost lives. That's the job of the Holy Spirit.

Our job is

- to believe what we've been called to believe;
- to obey his command to go to the four corners of the earth, telling people what God has done in Christ;

- to pray that the Holy Spirit would open hearts and minds when we tell others this Good News; and
- to trust that the God who has proven himself perfectly just and perfectly merciful on the cross will accomplish his will through us and sometimes in spite of us.

This is freedom: accepting what has been revealed and living in trusting obedience. The God who opened the disciples' eyes on the road to Emmaus and who appeared to Saul on his journey is the same God who can be trusted to open hearts and minds today.

CHAPTER 5

The Point of Heaven

I REMEMBER DREADING the first Thanksgiving our family celebrated after my mother died. All her life, my mother had been the catalyst for gathering cousins and aunts and uncles on that day. Joy and laughter permeated the get-togethers my mom organized because she was the proverbial life of the party. Having lived with her, I knew she wasn't always so upbeat. But when she was with people, and the event was a special occasion, my mom had a way of helping everyone celebrate.

So we wondered what it was going to be like having our Thanksgiving without her. All of us—cousins and aunts and so forth—gathered as we usually did. The food was wonderful, the jokes were funny, the conversation was engaging. It was still a lot of fun. But something was missing. *Someone* was missing. We went through all the motions of a Thanksgiving holiday, but because my mother wasn't there, it wasn't the same.

The vision of heaven in *Love Wins* is a vision of the celebration of life—life as we know it, but even better. It's something we'll enjoy together, something that will be very much like life as we know it today. This is a wonderful vision, one that whets our appetite and is in line with Scripture in many respects. The only problem is that in the version of heaven portrayed in *Love Wins*, someone is more or less missing from the picture.

To see what I mean, we need to look at how the Bible describes heaven.

Heaven's Dimensions

When we speak of the biblical heaven, there is more than one thing we might be referring to.

Sometimes *heaven* just means sky, as when people look up into the heavens.[32]

As *Love Wins* points out, *heaven* is sometimes used as merely another name for God. We find that especially in Matthew's Gospel, where the Kingdom of God is regularly called the Kingdom of Heaven.[33]

Heaven is also used to describe the reality where God rules, a place that is filled with God in unmistakable ways. Thus Jesus can pray that God's will be done on earth *as it is in heaven* (see Matthew 6:10). Wherever this heaven is, it is not earth.[34]

Regardless of its location, heaven seems to be the place where the faithful go immediately after they die. It's often called by other names, but the idea is the same. At one point, Jesus tells the disciples that he will be leaving them but that he is going to prepare a place for them (see John 14:2). Paul tells the church in Philippi that if he were to die, he would immediately be "with Christ" (Philippians 1:23). Heaven is what is being alluded to in both instances—heaven as a place where God fills all in all.

This other place, where God rules and where his people end up, is what most people mean when they talk about heaven. It's an understanding that is limited, to be sure. But it is not as distorted as many recent books, including *Love Wins*, would lead us to believe. Our ultimate destiny is the new heavens and a new earth (see Isaiah 65:17; Revelation 21:1), which is a much more tangible existence than we sometimes imagine. But on a day-to-day basis, what concerns most of us is, What will happen immediately after I die? Will I go to heaven? And by that we really do mean someplace other than here on earth.

Since both Jesus and Paul acknowledge this dimension of heaven, it is not inaccurate to think of heaven as someplace else—a destination to be arrived at. We must not forget how central the idea of faith as a journey is in Scripture, like Abraham's journey from Ur or the Israelites' journey to the land of milk and honey. The idea that we are pilgrims moving to another location—to a place called the Promised Land or heaven—encompasses some important biblical themes.

And whether we're talking about the place we go immediately after we die or the Kingdom that God will ultimately establish, the intermediate heaven or the ultimate heaven on earth, what they both have in common is this: God is at the center. God is what heaven is all about.

A Tangible Heaven

Love Wins draws a striking, if limited, picture of our ultimate destiny and the ultimate destiny of the planet—the Kingdom of Heaven that will be incarnated on earth.

Love Wins does that first by trying to help us grasp what the Bible means by *the age to come* and *eternal life*. It tries to prove that these phrases don't mean "eternity" or "forever and ever" but an "intensity of experience that transcends time."[35] But the book's exegesis (or interpretation) of these points has been universally criticized. Take *eternal life*, for instance: no lexicon of the Greek language defines the Greek word *aion* as an "intensity of experience that transcends time."

Nonetheless, the larger point about the concreteness of the Kingdom of Heaven is well taken. To that end, *Love Wins* quotes Old Testament passages that use tangible metaphors to describe the future age:

- How the earth (not heaven, as such) "will be filled with the knowledge of the LORD" (Isaiah 11:9, NIV)

- That it will be like enjoying a rich feast
  (see Isaiah 25:6, NIV)
- That people will be given grain and fruit and crops
  along with new hearts (see Ezekiel 36:26-30, NIV)
- That "new wine will drip from the mountains"
  (Amos 9:13, NIV)

"If this sounds like heaven on earth," it sums up, "that's because it is. Literally."[36]

The book then points out three particular characteristics of this heaven on earth: (1) It includes people of all nations and cultures and races. (2) It is earthy and tangible. (3) The purpose of life there will be "to participate, to partner with God in taking the world somewhere." By that it means, "God has been looking for partners . . . who will take seriously their divine responsibility to care for the earth and each other in loving, sustainable ways."[37]

For this to happen, there has to be a judgment. "For the earth to be free of anything destructive or damaging, certain things have to be banished."[38] Things like war, rape, greed, pride, exploitation, and so forth, are all summed up in the book by the word *injustice*. *Love Wins* says that in the Kingdom of Heaven justice will reign. It also adds that we all live with the "haunting thought" about how "our own sins have contributed to the heartbreak we're surrounded by." But that there is mercy, too, for God will forgive those sins.[39]

According to *Love Wins*, the question is, "How do you

make sure you'll be a part of the new thing God is going to do? How do you best become the kind of person whom God could entrust with significant responsibility in the age to come?"

The answer it gives is, "The more you become a person of peace and justice and worship and generosity, the more actively you participate now in ordering and working to bring about God's kind of world, the more ready you will be to assume an even greater role in the age to come."[40]

Love Wins unpacks the Bible story of the rich young ruler to talk about these prerequisites for gaining eternal life. It eventually concludes that the decisive moment in the conversation is when Jesus asks the man to sell his possessions. Only by doing this, says the book, will he be opened up "to more and more participation in God's new world."[41]

At this point we need to focus on what seem to me to be serious (if inadvertent) distortions of the gospel. What is being described here is a near-perfect example of works-based righteousness. According to *Love Wins*, in order to be ready to live in heaven, one has to become a certain type of person and work "to bring about God's kind of world." There is not a word in the book about the nature of faith and the radical grace that makes such a life possible in Jesus.

To be sure, some passages in the Gospels and in the Epistles say we will be judged by how we live our lives. But the church has always taught that these passages are to be read in light of ones like these:

> *God presented Jesus as the sacrifice for sin. People are*
> *made right with God when they believe that Jesus*
> *sacrificed his life, shedding his blood.*
>
> (ROMANS 3:25)

> *If you confess with your mouth that Jesus is Lord and*
> *believe in your heart that God raised him from the*
> *dead, you will be saved.*
>
> (ROMANS 10:9)

We are made ready for heaven by the death and resurrection of Jesus Christ, which we participate in by faith, not by anything we do or achieve.

But, of course, the New Testament also teaches that good works will naturally flow out of salvation:

> *God saved you by his grace when you believed. And*
> *you can't take credit for this; it is a gift from God.*
> *Salvation is not a reward for the good things we have*
> *done, so none of us can boast about it. For we are God's*
> *masterpiece. He has created us anew in Christ Jesus, so*
> *we can do the good things he planned for us long ago.*
>
> (EPHESIANS 2:8-10)

Some of those good things, as *Love Wins* says, include "working to bring about God's kind of world." But it is not working that prepares a place for us in heaven; it is Jesus who prepares the place, through his death and resurrection, by the grace of the Holy Spirit.

Because *Love Wins* fails to mention in this context any

connection to Jesus' work or person, it will likely create serious misunderstanding. Some readers will naturally assume that it is what we do that makes all the difference. But in fact, even in the discussion of Jesus' invitation to the rich young ruler, the accent falls on the very last thing Jesus tells him: "Follow me" (Matthew 19:21). It's not about what we do but about *who* we follow.

Unfortunately, *Love Wins* doesn't even note this phrase from this story. Of course, to follow Jesus means to trust Jesus, and to trust Jesus means to obey Jesus. But it is *Jesus*—not the selling of possessions—who will open us up to participation in God's new world. It is grace through faith that leads to obedience—all focused on the work of Christ on the cross— that is at the heart of the gospel.

What Heaven Is About

When answering the question "What will we do in heaven?" *Love Wins* says:

> What do you love to do now that will go on in the world to come? What is it that when you do it, you lose track of time because you get lost in it? What do you do that makes you think, "I could do this forever"? What is it that makes you think, "I was made for this"?[42]

Again,

> Heaven is both the peace, stillness, serenity, and calm that come from having everything in its right

place . . . and the endless joy that comes from participating in the ongoing creation of the world.[43]

But, *Love Wins* continues, "Jesus makes no promise that in the blink of an eye we will suddenly become totally different people who have vastly different tastes, attitudes, and perspectives." The book claims that "heaven has the potential to be a kind of starting over. Learning how to be human all over again." That includes "constantly learning and growing and evolving and absorbing."[44]

Here we must stop yet again to note how this compares to the fuller biblical picture. Yes, heaven will be a place where we will, in fact, enjoy the fruits of living in the new heaven and the new earth. We'll bask in the fellowship of others and likely even work together to create and fashion a beautiful and interesting world. We will continue to grow ever more into the image of Christ. According to Scripture, that seems to be part and parcel of life in heaven (see Ezekiel 28:24-26; Isaiah 49:8-11; Revelation 22:3-5).

But in general, the Bible devotes relatively little space talking about what we'll do with one another in heaven or what our creative heavenly work will be like. Instead, Scripture talks about heaven as though its most important feature— the most glorious thing there—is God. Take, for example, the vision given to Isaiah:

> *In the last days, the mountain of the LORD's house*
> *will be the highest of all—*
> *the most important place on earth.*

It will be raised above the other hills,
    and people from all over the world will stream there
        to worship.
People from many nations will come and say,
"Come, let us go up to the mountain of the LORD,
    to the house of Jacob's God.
There he will teach us his ways,
    and we will walk in his paths."

(ISAIAH 2:2-3)

The Kingdom of Heaven is wonderful not because of what we get to do but because the Lord is there and because he will teach us. Or take this passage from Revelation, which assumes that the central activity of heaven will not be creativity or work, but the worship of God:

Day after day and night after night they keep on saying,

"Holy, holy, holy is the Lord God, the Almighty—
    the one who always was, who is, and who is still
        to come."

Whenever the living beings give glory and honor and thanks to the one sitting on the throne (the one who lives forever and ever), the twenty-four elders fall down and worship the one sitting on the throne (the one who lives forever and ever). And they lay their crowns before the throne and say,

"You are worthy, O Lord our God,
*   to receive glory and honor and power.*
For you created all things,
*   and they exist because you created*
*   what you pleased."*

(REVELATION 4:8-11)

The main activity in this scene is the worship of God. In the chapter on heaven in *Love Wins*, the idea of worship in heaven is not pictured at all; the word *worship* appears only once, and then only in passing. Yet when the author of Revelation thinks of heaven, the first thing he describes is worship of God.

And then there is the climactic passage in the book of Revelation, which describes the new heaven and the new earth descending on the planet. And what is so wonderful about this?

I saw the holy city, the new Jerusalem, coming down
from God out of heaven like a bride beautifully dressed
for her husband. I heard a loud shout from the throne,
saying, "Look, God's home is now among his people! He
will live with them, and they will be his people. God
himself will be with them.

(REVELATION 21:2-3)

Only next comes a description of the impact on us—the promise that death and sorrow and crying and pain will be no more. The most glorious thing about heaven is that God himself will be with us.

Unfortunately, in *Love Wins*, just as Jesus seems to play no role in making us ready for heaven (except to give us commands), neither does God play a significant role in heaven. Yes, we are said to partner with him, but this idea is never explained, and it is only mentioned in passing in a discussion about what *we* do in heaven. We read repeatedly about how we'll feel in heaven (happy, peaceful, calm, joyful) and what we'll do (working, creating)—and usually both at the same time (doing what makes us the happiest). But there's hardly anything at all about heaven as a place where we fellowship with God face-to-face and worship him.

When *Love Wins* describes what the presence of God is like in heaven, it reverts to language that is regrettably impersonal and vague. *Love Wins* maintains that, in explaining the Kingdom of God,

[Jesus] described an all-pervasive dimension of being, a bit like oxygen for us or water for a fish. . . . He spoke of oneness with God, the God who is so intimately connected with life in this world that every hair on your head is known. Jesus lived and spoke as if the whole world was a thin place for him, with endless dimensions of the divine infinitesimally close, with every moment and every location simply another experience of the divine reality that is all around us.[45]

According to *Love Wins*, then, God's presence is a "dimension of being." It is all around us, but more like air for us or water for fish—vital but certainly not personal. The words used to describe God become increasingly vague as the paragraph goes on—"endless dimensions of the divine infinitesimally close" and a "divine reality that is all around us."

However, when Jesus speaks about God, he rarely reverts to impersonal, vague language. He never talks about God as a "dimension of being" or "the divine," and when he does use an analogy, more often than not God is compared to a person—a master or a shepherd or a woman who has lost a precious coin—not to air or water. When Jesus does use an inanimate object to describe himself, he turns it into an active metaphor: *living* water, bread that *feeds*. And more important, these images do not simply surround you; they penetrate your very being. So they end up being personal images after all.

When speaking about our relationship with God, Jesus again avoids the abstract and highlights the personal. Or better, he takes the abstract and makes it personal. For Jesus, his oneness with the Father is nothing less than love: "I love the Father" (John 14:31), and "I have loved you even as the Father has loved me" (John 15:9). To be one means to be in a deeply personal relationship.

I don't know why *Love Wins* feels compelled to downplay the presence of God in heaven and to talk about his presence in such vague and abstract language. The use of these descriptions makes one think of "the divine" as pictured in Eastern religions—all-pervasive but ultimately impersonal. I'm sure this is inadvertent in *Love Wins*, but it has the unhappy consequence of describing a deity who is not much like God the Father or Jesus Christ.

The Real Experience of Heaven

In the final section of the chapter on heaven, notably titled "Here Is the New There," *Love Wins* makes an argument that heaven begins today, that we can start enjoying a heavenly life in this life.

> When Jesus talked about heaven, he was talking about our present, *eternal, intense, real* experiences of joy, peace, and love in this life. . . . Heaven for Jesus wasn't just "someday"; it was a present reality.[46]

Here again, *Love Wins* addresses an important biblical theme. If we're living only for a pie-in-the-sky by and by, we're not living the Christian life described in the Bible. For there is something of heaven we can already begin to participate in right now. But again, *Love Wins* focuses on the self and what the self feels. Heaven is about "experiences of joy, peace, and love."

For Jesus, heaven is about our personal and intimate connection with him, just as he has a personal and intimate connection with the Father (see John 10:28-30; 17:22-24). It is about the *reality* of our being one with him and with the Father.

In contrast to *Love Wins*, Jesus rarely uses the language of experience to talk about this unity in love. There is no question that we will sometimes experience God as "joy, peace, and love." But Jesus' focus is on a new reality. Whether we happen to experience it or not at any given moment or period, whether we feel anything or not, he promises that those who put their trust in him now have a personal and *real* connection with him and the Father.

If there is an emotion that increasingly characterizes the Christian life, it is one that is, paradoxically, focused outside ourselves: a yearning and desire *for God*. Not a desire for joy and peace and meaningful work to do forever, but a desire for God.

The Psalms are especially expressive of the emotional contours of the Christian life, now and in heaven. The following psalm paints a striking picture of how pervasive and relentless this yearning can be:

O God, you are my God;
I earnestly search for you.
My soul thirsts for you;
my whole body longs for you
in this parched and weary land
where there is no water.
I have seen you in your sanctuary
and gazed upon your power and glory.
Your unfailing love is better than life itself;
how I praise you!

I will praise you as long as I live,
*   lifting up my hands to you in prayer.*
You satisfy me more than the richest feast.
*   I will praise you with songs of joy.*

I lie awake thinking of you,
*   meditating on you through the night.*
Because you are my helper,
*   I sing for joy in the shadow of your wings.*
I cling to you;
*   your strong right hand holds me securely.*
            (PSALM 63:1-8)

There are many contrasts between the psalmist's perspective and the *Love Wins* vision of heaven, but perhaps the most poignant is this: "Your unfailing love is better than life itself." By *love*, the psalmist clearly means something personal and intimate, something a soul thirsts for and a body aches for. *God himself*—not the life activities he gives us to enjoy—is the psalmist's passion.

God's relentless passion for unity with us is evident throughout the Bible, from the moment when our relationship with God is broken and he calls out, "Adam, where are you?" to the fulfillment of the biblical hope, when God comes to live face-to-face among his people. Then, among other things, we will spend eternity beholding his beauty and glory and worshiping him with great shouts of praise.

CHAPTER 6

Hell and Judgment

AT ONE POINT in the movie *Patton*, General Omar Bradley tells General George Patton that Patton may be given a crucial assignment: leading troops in the invasion of Europe.[47] At the time, though he had played a decisive role in the battle for Africa and in the invasion of Sicily, Patton is cooling his heels in England, being disciplined for making careless remarks and slapping a soldier in a field hospital. So he's anxious to get back into the thick of battle, and when he hears about the possible assignment, he can hardly contain himself.

But then General Bradley tells him no decision has been made, that it's in yet another general's hands. Patton has a history of being an aggressive soldier, taking initiative while others stand around deliberating their course of action. He is not the sort of man who likes to leave his fate to the judgment of someone else.

We are a lot like Patton when it comes to questions about heaven and hell. We want answers—and we want them now. We don't want to wait for deliberations or meetings or half answers. It's the eternal fates of our neighbors and friends we are talking about. We wonder how a good God could even allow a hell. *Is the Last Judgment really final? Does it happen at the point of death, or sometime afterward?* We worry about the eternal fate of loved ones who never believed and about those who believed and then abandoned their faith. *Are they in hell? Does hell really last for eternity?* So troubling are such questions that some people are tempted to take the initiative and start deciding the answers themselves.

Love Wins is to be given credit for facing the tough issues of hell and judgment. It's rare for churches to address these topics, and when they do, they often talk about them in ways that are not particularly biblical. Unfortunately, this is one of the problems we find in *Love Wins*, too. In fact, I found the arguments in its chapter on hell to be the most incoherent in the book. The problems stem partly from misunderstandings about what the Bible means by certain words and ideas, and partly from assumptions that drive the discussion itself.

We'll get to all that in this chapter, but first, we need a brief overview of the Bible's teaching on hell and judgment to set everything in context.

Hell

The Greek word that we translate as "hell" is *Gehenna*. It comes from the Hebrew word for the Valley of Hinnom, or Ben-Hinnom, a valley that lies outside Jerusalem (see Joshua 15:8). It was infamous for being the place where children had been sacrificed by fire in pagan rituals (see 2 Chronicles 28:3). There is no clear proof that it was ever a garbage dump where refuse was burned. Still, over time Gehenna also became the name of the place where sinners were punished after death.

In the New Testament, the suffering of hell is mostly pictured as fire (see Mark 9:43) but also as darkness (see Matthew 25:30; 2 Peter 2:17) and as destruction and exclusion from the presence of the Lord (see 2 Thessalonians 1:9; Matthew 7:21-23). The point is less to describe hell in detail than to suggest it is a place of torment.

It can be safely assumed from Scripture that hell is just as everlasting as heaven (see Matthew 25:46). There is no talk anywhere in the New Testament of people ever leaving hell. The longest and most widely held view is that those in hell experience torment for eternity, and there remain strong arguments for this view. Some evangelicals, including John Stott, believe there is a biblical case to be made for annihilationism—the theory that at some point those in hell experience "the second death" (Revelation 20), or what is also called eternal destruction. That is, their existence simply ceases, and they suffer eternal consequences in the sense that not the punishment but the consequence lasts forever.

Annihilationism remains a minority view, but in either case, the consequences of rejecting God last for eternity.

The doctrine of hell, like most others, comes packaged with other ideas that can't be separated from it. The most important is the Last Judgment.

Judgment

The idea of God as "Judge of all the earth" appears early in the Bible (Genesis 18:25). God "will judge the world with justice and rule the nations with fairness" (Psalm 9:8). His judgment includes both punishment for the wicked and reward for the faithful:

> *I, the LORD, love justice.*
> *I hate robbery and wrongdoing.*
> *I will faithfully reward my people for their suffering*
> *and make an everlasting covenant with them.*
> (ISAIAH 61:8)

While many of the verses in Proverbs speak of the natural consequences of bad behavior (see Proverbs 5:22-23; 6:27-29; 9:12, for instance), God's judgment is personal, something God himself executes:

> *The Lord will wash the filth from beautiful Zion*
> *and cleanse Jerusalem of its bloodstains*
> *with the hot breath of fiery judgment.*
> (ISAIAH 4:4)

Many people think the Old Testament is the testament of judgment and the New Testament the testament of grace. That distinction is true in only a limited sense; in fact, the New Testament intensifies the Old Testament ideas of judgment. Similarly, many believe that in the Old Testament we witness a judging God but in the New Testament a merciful Jesus. In the New Testament, however, judgment now becomes associated closely with Jesus himself. The fact that in the New Testament the judge has become Jesus is a crucial factor to note, for it will affect how we understand many of the questions that swirl around hell and judgment.

The Last Judgment is a major theme in the parables of Jesus (see Matthew 13:24-30, 36-43, 47-50; 21:33-41; 22:1-14; 25:1-13, 31-46, among others). In the Gospel of John, in which Jesus talks so much about God's love, Jesus also says that he acts in God's stead in this capacity: God "has given the Son absolute authority to judge" (John 5:22) and, "I judge as God tells me. Therefore, my judgment is just, because I carry out the will of the one who sent me, not my own will" (John 5:30).

In the New Testament, God's judgment has already begun in some respects. His wrath is already evident in the way he allows sin to multiply and intensify (see Romans 1:18-32). But the overall focus is on the future judgment, and again, this judgment is associated with Christ (see Acts 10:42), for it will accompany the return of Christ (see Matthew 25:31-33; 2 Timothy 4:1).

All people, including Christians, will be subject to the Last Judgment, and every aspect of life will be judged—not just actions, but even motives (see 1 Corinthians 4:5). But for Christians, the Last Judgment is something they can nonetheless look forward to, for that will be the day when their faith in Christ is vindicated and their blamelessness in Christ is revealed (see 1 Corinthians 1:8; 2 Timothy 4:8).

> *As we live in God, our love grows more perfect. So we will not be afraid on the day of judgment, but we can face him with confidence because we live like Jesus here in this world.*
>
> (1 JOHN 4:17)

That is the basic overview of the biblical teaching on hell and judgment. There are, of course, nuances and differing interpretations about secondary matters. Certain elements of hell and judgment have been exaggerated here and there, and some biblical images (like fire) have become inordinately dominant in Western culture. But the main truths are clear, and they have constituted the teaching of the church from the beginning. As the fourth-century Nicene Creed puts it, Christ "will come again in glory to judge the living and the dead, and his kingdom will have no end."

A Judge We Can Trust

Such teaching makes us feel uncomfortable. Some Christians are so unsure of their standing with God that the mere thought of judgment frightens them. Others are not so much concerned about themselves as for their loved ones who have never put their trust in Christ—how will they avoid hell? Still others, as we see in *Love Wins*, think hell and judgment reflect badly on God and want to protect his reputation. So it's understandable that we are tempted to soften the Bible's teaching on hell and judgment.

But if we are going to be faithful to what God has revealed to us about hell, we are wise to stick to his revelation—the truths he has communicated to us in Scripture. The key New Testament revelation about judgment is that it is now connected with the person of Jesus Christ. And that makes all the difference.

To be sure, the person doing the judging is not one to be trifled with. He is not "Jesus meek and mild," with no moral backbone. John the Baptist describes Jesus as one who would baptize not only with water but with fire—that's backbone. Jesus himself said that he came not to bring merely peace but also a sword. In his ministry, Jesus had no patience with self-righteousness and hypocrisy. He took a whip to those who desecrated holy places. He made extraordinary demands on those who would follow him, saying that faith in him required nothing less than their death.[48]

But this same Jesus, the one who will be our judge, also welcomed into his company the corrupt tax collector Zacchaeus, the woman caught in adultery, prostitutes, and other assorted sinners. He invited one and all with comforting words like, "Come to me, all of you who are weary and carry heavy burdens, and I will give you rest" (Matthew 11:28) and "I am leaving you with a gift—peace of mind and heart. And the peace I give is a gift the world cannot give. So don't be troubled or afraid" (John 14:27).

And most crucially, the one who will be our judge went to the cross to condemn evil, sin, and death—to give them their just deserts—and to make possible for us the forgiveness of sins and reconciliation with God. The same Jesus who has shown himself to be perfectly just and perfectly merciful is the one who will carry out the judgment. We can have complete confidence in him to do what is right and good on that day.

Let's return to the movie *Patton* once more to consider what happens just after General Patton hears that his fate lies in the hands of General George Marshall. Patton responds somewhat unexpectedly: he actually calms down. Not fond of leaving his future in someone else's control, he nevertheless finds confidence in knowing General Marshall's character: "He's a good man," Patton says. "At least he's a fair man. I'll let it sit with him."

This representation of the gruff old general actually paints a pretty clear picture for us, suggesting the biblical response that even a fiercely autonomous people like us can have. We can rightly assume that when it comes to hell and the Last Judgment, Jesus is more than fair and good—even perfectly just and loving. We can in confidence let all our questions and concerns "sit with him." This is the assumption with which we should begin all conversations about hell and judgment. When we don't begin here, we will inevitably get ourselves into all sorts of trouble, as does *Love Wins*.

Telling the Right Story

The discussion about hell and judgment in *Love Wins* hinges on a problem about what God is like. The problem is presented like this:

> God is loving and kind and full of grace and mercy—unless there isn't confession and repentance and salvation in this lifetime, at which point God punishes forever. That's the Christian story, right? [49]

Thus the chapter attempts to retell this story. But one can already see that beginning the chapter this way sets it off on a troublesome course. For one thing, the story it summarizes is *not* the Christian story. The Christian story moves in precisely the opposite direction.

In that story, all of us are lost and doomed to eternal death because of our sin and rebellion against God. But instead of leaving us with no recourse but to suffer the just consequences of our sin, he comes in Christ to reconcile us to himself. Through the ministry of the Holy Spirit, we are now invited to be reconciled to God through repentance and faith. If we do not become reconciled to God, nothing changes. We continue on a course that was already set by our sin and disobedience. But the good news is that we don't have to stay on that trajectory!

That's the Christian story. The so-called Christian story that *Love Wins* sets up is a distortion. To be sure, some

Christians have misconstrued the story in that way. But the way to correct that problem is by telling the Christian story in the right way, not by trying to tell a whole new story. As might be expected, as the book begins to retell that story, it makes a series of blunders, all of which have been pointed out in the many reviews of the book.

For example, *Love Wins* begins by exploring the meaning of the word *hell* in the Old and New Testaments. According to the book, the Old Testament view of what happens after a person dies "isn't very articulated or defined . . . a bit vague and 'underworldly.'"[50]

> For whatever reasons, the precise details of who goes
> where, when, how, with what, and for how long
> simply aren't things the Hebrew writers were terribly
> concerned with.[51]

The Hebrew writers were God's prophets, who were by definition God's mouthpieces. They spoke and wrote down only the messages God wanted to send to his people at that time and in that place. God revealed most of the details we know about hell later, in the New Testament period. It's God's prerogative to reveal what he wants us to know—and when. It's also true that the New Testament doesn't talk in detail about hell, but through Jesus' words and other New Testament writers, God reveals enough about it to suggest that it is something we should indeed be concerned with. So what's important is how we will respond to what God has revealed to us in his Word—not when it was revealed or how many details we have about it.

Hell Today?

Love Wins goes on to argue that hell can be understood as the sufferings we bring on ourselves today. It describes the Rwanda genocide, in which machete-wielding men killed and maimed the innocent. It mentions women who have been raped, a child whose father committed suicide, and a bitterly vindictive man who left nothing of his estate to his loved ones in order to hurt them.

The book uses the effects of these unquestionably evil actions to drive home the point that we create our own hells by rejecting the goodness of God and perpetrating evil. The suffering caused by our choices creates a hell for us.

The problem is this: in the illustrations used to support this point, it is the victims who suffer hellish consequences. In these examples, those who have chosen evil do not suffer— not even from guilt. So it seems an incoherent conclusion to draw from these examples that "God gives us what we want, and if that's hell, we can have it."[52] None of the sufferers in these examples have chosen hell, but it has been nonetheless brought upon them.

There is something right in the idea that the judgment of God is visited upon people in this life to some degree. Paul speaks of this in Romans: "God shows his anger from heaven against all sinful, wicked people who suppress the truth by their wickedness" (Romans 1:18). He then explains that in this life, God's judgment is manifest through the consequences of sin.

We see that played out in many instances. The wrecked life of the drug addict. The way lies create more problems than they solve. How adultery can destroy a marriage. But there are two important things to notice about the situations we get ourselves in.

First, a lot of people commit horrendous sins and never suffer consequences for them in this life. There are men and women in the highest echelons of Wall Street and Pennsylvania Avenue whose dishonesty and mismanagement caused the great recession of 2008, and yet they still live in luxury and freedom. There are dictators who cruelly oppress their people and still reign unopposed. There are sex traffickers enslaving innocent children and getting away with it year after year. There are serial killers who are never caught. The empirical fact is that for many people, there is no hell in this life.

Second, when we do commit sins that create a hell in our lives, these sins inevitably bring hell to other people's lives as well. Take drug addiction. It affects not only addicts, but their spouses, their children, their coworkers, their friends—all of whom suffer because of their choices. Adultery deeply affects the spouse, not just the one committing adultery, and it may very well impact children, friends, and family in a ripple effect.

In other words, it is simply absurd to say that in this life we choose our hells, or that the hells we experience are due to our choices. Life just doesn't work that way. This is precisely why the idea of judgment is stressed in Scripture and remains a compelling doctrine in the Christian faith. Many wicked people create hells for others but suffer no consequences in this life. The answer is that God is just, so there is a consequence for such behavior, but the consequence will not necessarily be felt until future judgment.

More Odd Exegesis

Love Wins next looks at Luke 16:19-31, the parable of the rich man and the poor beggar. In this parable the rich man goes to Hades, but the poor man goes to be with Abraham, meaning he goes to heaven. The rich man wants mercy and water to cool his tongue, because as he says, "I am in anguish in these flames."

Abraham tells the rich man that not only did he have his chance in this life, but now "there is a great chasm separating us. No one can cross over to you from here, and no one can cross over to us from there." So the rich man begs Abraham to send a message to his family to warn them "so they don't end up in this place of torment." Abraham replies that they've got Moses and the prophets, and they can listen to them; he also says even if someone were raised from the dead and spoke to them, they would not be convinced.

According to *Love Wins*, the problem in this parable is that the rich man wants the poor man to serve him. And the great chasm is "the rich man's heart . . . [which] hasn't changed. . . . He's still clinging to the old hierarchy."[53] For *Love Wins*, the parable is foremost about social equality.

This is an intriguing interpretation. But it's simply not supported by a plain reading of the parable. First, it might be plausible that the rich man is still thinking of Lazarus as beneath him—except that he seems to realize that Lazarus has made it to heaven, while he is in hell. Second, the overall message is not about equality; it's about showing mercy to those who suffer in this life. The chasm is not in the rich man's heart but between those who suffer in hell and those who enjoy heaven. And the point of the parable is ultimately not even about heaven and hell; it's about Jesus. It is shaped to teach that some people are so unmerciful and hardened, they won't believe in Jesus even if he should rise from the dead.

Time and again, where *Love Wins* attempts to retell the biblical story, it results in a serious misrepresentation of the real story.

What Type of Judgment

The book then moves on to an extended discussion of judgment, noting how the many warnings about God's judgment of Israel are accompanied by promises of restoration. It concludes, "Failure, we see again and again, isn't final, judgment has a point, and consequences are for correction."[54]

Also noted are the many instances in which judgment is used in a human way to bring people to repentance, as when Paul, referring to one notorious sinner, tells the church at Corinth, "You must throw this man out and hand him over to Satan so that his sinful nature will be destroyed and he himself will be saved on the day the Lord returns" (1 Corinthians 5:5). In other words, "Paul is convinced . . . that wrongdoers will become right doers"[55] through such judgment.

Finally, *Love Wins* talks about the Greek words that get translated as "eternal destruction," which is often the way the Bible talks about the Last Judgment. It argues that *aion* (usually translated as "eternal") can also mean "age" or "period of time." *Kolazo* (usually translated as "destruction") can mean "pruning" or "trimming." Thus an *aion* of *kolazo* likely does not mean "eternal destruction" but probably "a period of pruning" or a "time of intense trimming."[56]

Unfortunately—again—this is creative exegesis. Greek dictionaries define *kalazo* as "infliction of chastisement," "punishment," "transcendent retribution." The verb form means "to penalize, punish." New Testament scholar Scot McKnight says on his blog commentary on this chapter, "There is very little emphasis in this word's usage that suggests punish to improve."[57] These words in the New Testament, he says, are used to talk about punishment in the age to come, and the age to come is everlasting.

Love Wins then argues that in the parable of the sheep and the goats (see Matthew 25:31-46), *eternal* in "eternal punishment" for the goats must mean "for a long time," which must mean that at some point the punishment ends. But the same word, *aion*, is used in the phrase "eternal life." Does the book interpret this also as "a long time"? Does it mean to suggest that life in the Kingdom of Heaven will someday end as well?

I don't think that was the book's intended implication, but it makes no provision for another interpretation.

The Problem of Choice—Again

This brings us to the key issue in the *Love Wins* chapter on hell. I highlighted it in my chapter on faith, but we need to expand on that now because the *Love Wins* notions of choice and unqualified free will run into even deeper problems. To repeat, we read in this chapter that

> God gives us what we want, and if that's hell, we can have it. We have that kind of freedom, that kind of choice. We are that free.[58]

Much of the ensuing discussion is driven by this assumption and one other: that hell is a temporary place of punishment. This becomes obvious in the following chapter on universalism, where *Love Wins* leaves open the possibility that even in hell we can repent—make a new choice—and return to God. In other words, freedom to choose continues to be a reality in hell. There are two particular problems with this assumption.

First, one wonders what *Love Wins* means by "freedom" or "free choice" in the context of its conception of heaven and hell. If someone experiences the torment of hell but then, because of that torment, decides to love God, can we say that the decision was made in freedom? Hasn't that love been coerced by the pains of hell? And what about those who are enjoying heaven because of the joy and peace it brings: can it really be said that they are freely loving God? Aren't they being cajoled, manipulated into faith by divine blessings? Does freedom have any real meaning, then, in heaven and hell? And if not, can anyone be said to truly love God according to the book's definition of love?

Second, for the sake of argument, let's grant the assumption that people in hell still have true freedom to choose God: if people in hell still have this freedom, surely people in heaven still have freedom to choose. And if people in hell can for eternity still choose heaven, then it follows that even later in eternity they could choose hell again. And those in heaven to begin with, if they still have free choice, can choose hell anytime they want.

Now why would people choose hell after living in heaven? That's hard to imagine, but I would assume it would be for the same reason people choose to reject God's goodness and love in this life. After all, according to *Love Wins*, heaven is not a place where we have been transformed into a new creation. On the contrary, the book says that "Jesus makes no promise that in the blink of an eye we will suddenly become totally different people." Instead, heaven is a place of "learning and growing and evolving and absorbing."[59]

But how do we learn and grow in this life? It's usually because of mistakes we make, sins we commit, evils we perpetrate. That is, we tend to learn and grow because we temporarily reject the love and goodness of God and create our own little hells.

So given the *Love Wins* premise and assumptions about

life in heaven and hell and its absolute confidence in free choice, one can only assume that, yes, people in heaven can still choose hell. Not to worry, though, because they will suffer consequences if they do so, and they will again choose heaven. But they still are growing and learning, so they might choose hell again. It quickly becomes apparent that the vision of heaven and hell in *Love Wins* is not a vision of a future life but of life as it already is on earth. As with other unfortunate implications of the book's premise, I can't believe this is the intention of its author, but given those assumptions, we are left with no other conclusions to draw.

This is not the heaven and hell described in the Bible— both of which are eternal states. Nor is this the freedom the Bible talks about—which does not exist until the Holy Spirit works a miracle in our lives, and even then means only that we can now respond to God in faith. The *Love Wins* vision of heaven and hell does not reverberate with the astounding hope the Bible proclaims—that we will indeed be transformed into the very image of Christ, becoming eternally one in fellowship with God and others, never again to encounter the possibility or choice of sin, evil, sadness, and death (see 1 Corinthians 15:51-57; Revelation 21:4). In short, *Love Wins* in this regard does not give us the Good News of the gospel.

As for Those Questions

The idea that God will judge everyone and that the destiny of some people will be an eternal hell is unpalatable for most, and *Love Wins* clearly represents this perspective. Such a view denies that any judgment could be final, any existence in hell everlasting. It rejects the notion that an eternal hell is compatible with a God of love. And that is a key problem in the book. *Love Wins* grapples more with *the idea* of a God of love than with the God who has revealed himself in Jesus Christ or what that revealed love actually looks like.

According to Scripture, that revealed love looks like a cross. And on the cross we see not only God's infinite mercy but also his infinite justice: the God revealed in the Bible embraces both. In the Bible, it's not just love that wins but justice, too. Thus it is really better to say that *God* wins, since in Christ he accomplishes both.

Also revealed in the Bible, especially by the very one who will demonstrate perfect love and justice, are parable after parable about the final judgment and the eternal destruction of those who reject him.[60] Not only did Jesus himself make these themes central to his teaching but he also is revealed to be the one through whom the judgment will finally take place. In other words, God has plainly revealed to us that the Last Judgment and an eternal hell are realities that confront each of us.

But the Bible doesn't give us much beyond these few, bare truths. The exact nature of hell—fire? darkness? conscious torment? annihilation?—is not as clear. One other thing we are told is to never make judgments about who is in hell— we are not to judge, says Jesus (see Matthew 7). So even if we might wish that people like Hitler or bin Laden are in hell, we cannot know what might have happened just before they died. Might God give people an opportunity to repent immediately after they die but before they are judged? We might hope this is true, especially for those who have never heard of Jesus, for example. But we are simply not told how God deals with such people—whether bin Laden got a last-second chance to repent, as did the thief on the cross.

We do not know a lot about hell and the Last Judgment. What we do know is that there is an eternal hell and an eternal heaven and also that God has shown himself to be perfectly just and perfectly merciful in Jesus Christ. That means we can trust him to manage the affairs at the end of our lives in accord with his nature (see Psalm 131). We can let such matters lie with him. We do not have to reconcile paradoxes to which he has chosen not to reveal the solutions.

The trust we are called to put in God about the Last Judgment can begin with our trust in Jesus today. Anytime we wonder if we deserve eternal life with him, anytime we question whether we're good enough to be in his presence, anytime we're unsure of our faith, that's just the time we are invited to stop thinking about ourselves and look to Jesus Christ. As Paul puts it, "Christ has already accomplished the purpose for which the law was given. As a result, all who believe in him are made right with God" (Romans 10:4). It is Jesus—not our ability to make good choices—that assures us of everlasting life in heaven with him and the Father.

CHAPTER 7

The Bad News: Universalism

ONE LETTER sent to *Christianity Today* in March 2011, just after the *Love Wins* controversy exploded, sums up a dilemma many people, including devout Christians, feel deep in their bones:

> If your God is perfect and all-powerful and loving, then why does he not give everyone on this earth a fair chance to know him and accept him? An example of this is a kid in Iran born into a Muslim extremist family and taught that Islam is the one true religion and that Christianity is a lie. These kids do not get a fair chance at knowing God, and they go to hell and suffer for it eternally. That is extremely

unfair, and if that is the case, God is not perfect
but cruel.

Similar questions drive much of the message of *Love Wins*:

Of all the billions of people who have ever lived,
will only a select number "make it to a better place"
and every single other person suffer in torment
and punishment forever? Is this acceptable to God?
Has God created millions of people over tens of
thousands of years who are going to spend eternity
in anguish? Can God do this, or even allow this, and
still claim to be a loving God?[61]

These questions come at the beginning of the book, but
their force is felt throughout, most strongly in the chapter
"Does God Get What God Wants?" There *Love Wins* suggests
that "hard and fast, definitive declarations . . . about how God
will or will not organize the new world must leave plenty of
room for all kinds of . . . possibilities."[62] And the possibility the
book never commits to but is most aligned with is universalism: the teaching that all people will eventually be saved.

This is one of the most controversial aspects of *Love Wins*.
Before the book was even released, people started debating
whether its author is a universalist. I would argue that the point
is not whether Rob Bell is a universalist but whether universalism is an adequate or a biblical response to the questions raised
above. That's what will be addressed in this chapter.

An Argument from Desire

Regardless of the ultimate viewpoint of its author, *Love Wins* does attempt to justify the legitimacy of universalism. It does so in a variety of ways, first by pitting God's sovereignty against God's love. In the form of a syllogism, the logical argument looks something like this:

God is all-powerful; he can get whatever he wants.
God wants all to be saved.
Therefore, God gets what he wants—right?

The apparent contradiction this reveals is put more baldly this way:

Will all people be saved, or will God not get what God wants?[63]

The conclusion *Love Wins* clearly wants us to entertain is that, yes, God gets what he wants, so all people may very well be saved. But the logic is faulty. Does God get what he wants? Yes, of course; he's the all-powerful God. The question is, *what* does God want? Indeed, as 1 Timothy says, he "wants everyone to be saved and to understand the truth" (1 Timothy 2:3-4). But is that *all* God wants? Is that all the Bible tells us about what God desires? And is that the highest desire of God's heart?

As all the books of the prophets attest, God also wants

justice. This divine desire is aptly summed up in a simple verse from Isaiah: "I, the LORD, love justice. I hate robbery and wrongdoing" (Isaiah 61:8). God's sense of justice is not merely concerned with earthly matters; it also extends into the next life. We noted in the previous chapter how much the Last Judgment permeates both the Old and New Testaments, and how Jesus takes on the role of divine judge himself.

So we might ask, If God is all-powerful, and God wants to destroy all sin and those who perpetrate it, will God get what he wants? If so, none of us have any hope, for we are all sinners. But there are other things God wants. He is also said to want to demonstrate his glory:

> *Bring all who claim me as their God,*
> *for I have made them for my glory.*
> *It was I who created them.*
>
> (ISAIAH 43:7)

So we might ask, If God is all-powerful, and God wants his glory to shine forth, will God get what he wants? Again, yes, but we have to talk about what it means for God's glory to shine forth.

We could go on and on like this, because the Bible notes many things that God wants and loves. The question raised by *Love Wins* fails to account for *all* that God wants.

It also presumes that we can discern what God wants the most, as if we have a window into the inner sanctum of the Trinity, as if we can know the hidden counsels of God.

The point is that, when it comes to things eternal, we don't know all that God wants or what God wants most. He has revealed himself to us but not completely. "Just as the heavens are higher than the earth," he says, "so my ways are higher than your ways and my thoughts higher than your thoughts" (Isaiah 55:9).

We do know what God wants in relation to us—that all people come to a saving knowledge of Jesus Christ. But it's obvious from the Bible that there is something more that God wants, for the Bible clearly teaches about a Last Judgment and eternal consequences for rejecting him. We see that tension in a passage from the Gospels:

> As [Jesus] came closer to Jerusalem and saw the city
> ahead, he began to weep. "How I wish today that you
> of all people would understand the way to peace. But
> now it is too late, and peace is hidden from your eyes.
> Before long your enemies will build ramparts against
> your walls and encircle you and close in on you from
> every side. They will crush you into the ground, and
> your children with you. Your enemies will not leave a
> single stone in place, because you did not accept your
> opportunity for salvation."
>
> (LUKE 19:41-44)

Even on earth, God in Christ wants all Jerusalem to be saved from its impending judgment as a nation, but that doesn't mean that the people's lack of faith will forestall it.

The principle holds true for eternal judgment as well. It's not easy to figure out what God ultimately wants, but it's clear what he wants for us—and what the consequences are for rejecting him.

The History of Universalism

We have seen that *Love Wins* is open to universalism, even if that term is not actually used. Along this line, it says,

> And so, beginning with the early church, there is a
> long tradition of Christians who believe that God
> will ultimately restore everything and everybody.[64]

The book says that Clement of Alexandria and Origen "affirmed God's reconciliation with all people," as did Gregory of Nyssa and Eusebius. It also quotes Luther on the possibility that people could turn to God after death: "Who would doubt God's ability to do that?"[65]

But on these points the book is quite misleading and, in some cases, misinformed.

For one, universalism has indeed been around a long time, but throughout Christian history it has been decidedly in the minority. It was condemned by the early universal church council that met at Constantinople in 543. The view has not found favor with any significant theologian of the church since, including Martin Luther. It has been adopted by some Christians here and there, like George

Macdonald and William Law, but one can count on one's hands the number of prominent Christians who have held this view through the ages. It has been rejected by Orthodox Christians, Roman Catholics, and Protestants, and there is good reason for that.

As for Clement and Gregory, it is a matter of historical debate whether they were universalists. And the Luther quote, as many others have pointed out, was pulled out of context. Here is the larger context:

> If God were to save anyone without faith, he would
> be acting contrary to his own words and would give
> himself the lie; yes, he would deny himself. And that
> is impossible for, as St. Paul declares, God cannot
> deny himself (2 Timothy 2:13). It is as impossible
> for God to save without faith as it is impossible for
> divine truth to lie. . . . It would be quite a different
> question whether God can impart faith to some in
> the hour of death or after death so that these people
> could be saved through faith. *Who would doubt God's
> ability to do that?* No one, however, can prove that
> he does do this. For all that we read is that he has
> already raised people from the dead and thus granted
> them faith. But whether he gives faith or not, it is
> impossible for anyone to be saved without faith.
> Otherwise every sermon, the gospel, and faith would
> be vain, false, and deceptive, since the entire gospel
> makes faith necessary.[66]

In short, Luther wasn't simply saying that, because we don't know whether God chooses to inspire and accept faith after death, we can assume he does. No, he was saying that, because the Bible teaches nothing about conversion after death, faith in this life is crucial for salvation.

All in all, *Love Wins* tries to make universalism a legitimate option because "the Christian faith is big enough, wide enough, and generous enough to handle that vast a range of perspectives."[67] Yes, but only up to a point if it's going to have any integrity as a faith. The Christian faith certainly can have a number of perspectives on issues of secondary importance, and it does. But after twenty centuries of Christian thought, the central teachings of the faith have emerged relatively unscathed. They have been taught and affirmed by Christians of all traditions for a couple of thousand years. Universalism is not one of those teachings; it has been a belief ascribed to by only a minuscule number of Christians and has been rejected time and again by the church.

The reason for that rejection is the biblical witness. Not every hill of doctrine is one to die on, but on the central claims of the faith, the Bible is unambiguous. Early on the church summed up the biblical teaching on the Last Judgment when it affirmed in the Nicene Creed that Jesus Christ "will judge the living and the dead, and his kingdom shall have no end."

What Do You Mean by *All*?

When the word *eternal* is attached to words like *punishment* or *destruction*, *Love Wins* bends over backward to find another meaning for the word. As we noted in chapter 6, its efforts are unsuccessful. But it's also interesting to note that, when the book strives to suggest an argument for universalism, it never explores whether the words *all* or *every* might actually mean that all will be saved.

For example, *Love Wins* quotes from Isaiah 52 that "all the ends of the earth will see the salvation of our God" (verse 10, NIV).[68] But in the most inclusive interpretation possible, this verse merely says that God's salvation will be recognized, not necessarily accepted, in every part of the planet. At the least, it says that someone in every part of the planet will be saved, not everyone in every part.

Similarly, *Love Wins* quotes from Scripture that every knee will bow to God and every tongue confess his lordship.[69] But even demons acknowledge that Jesus is Lord and shudder at the thought (see James 2:19). So this verse doesn't imply the salvation of all people, only the eventual universal recognition that Jesus is Lord.

Universalists quote many other passages with the word *all* in them, but in context, most of those really mean "all Israel" or "all kinds of people" or "both Jews and Gentiles" will be saved. One example is found in Romans: "God has imprisoned everyone in disobedience so he could have mercy on everyone" (Romans 11:32). Paul has been discussing the place of Jews and Gentiles in the scheme of salvation, so clearly the "all" here means both Jews and Gentiles—not all within each group.

To be sure, in some passages the intent does seem to be

"each and every person." For example, in 2 Corinthians 5:19 Paul says, "God was in Christ, reconciling the world to himself, no longer counting people's sins against them." That accords with Colossians 1:20, which says that through Christ "God reconciled everything to himself" and "made peace with everything in heaven and on earth by means of Christ's blood on the cross."

But such passages are simply rehearsing the standard message of salvation—that God indeed loves the whole world so much that he gave his only begotten Son. Paul continues the theme of salvation by saying, "He gave us this wonderful message of reconciliation. So we are Christ's ambassadors; God is making his appeal through us. We speak for Christ when we plead, 'Come back to God!'" (2 Corinthians 5:19-20). This is hardly universalism. God reconciles the world to himself and forgives people's sins through Christ's death on the cross, yes! While we were sinners Christ died for us—for all of us, yes! But a response is called for if we are to claim that forgiveness, to make that forgiveness a living reality. We are called to be reconciled to God, as Paul puts it here, and to do so by faith.

Love Wins also argues that God will not give up on people, even after they die, and will pursue them for ages and ages, trying to convince them to accept his love. The book notes the parables of the shepherd who seeks out the lost sheep, the woman who seeks out the lost coin, and the father who waits for his prodigal son. The section concludes, "The God that Jesus teaches us about doesn't give up until everything that was lost is found. This God simply doesn't give up. Ever."[70]

But as we read these parables in context, we see that the point is not that God never gives up in eternity but that God seeks the lost and that he does so in the person of Jesus.

There are many other interpretation problems in the chapter, and there isn't the space here to comment on each one. All in all, the exegesis in this part of the book, and in the chapter on hell, seems to date back to a trend that became popular a century and a half ago. In the 1800s there was a lot of discussion about what *eternal* means, for example. "In this century, however," according to Richard Bauckham, New Testament scholar and senior scholar at Ridley Hall, Cambridge, "exegesis has turned decisively against the universalist case. Few would now doubt that many [New Testament] texts clearly teach a *final* division of mankind into saved and lost."[71]

As Bauckham also notes, despite the exegetical evidence, even some conservative theologians today hope for universal salvation. But of course, this is hardly inappropriate. If God wishes all to be saved, surely we who love God and want what he wants should hope for the salvation of all as well. But we cannot confuse a pious hope with the biblical teaching we are called to proclaim to all.

Divine Math

Finally, we need to look at a couple of theological assumptions that drive the *Love Wins* chapter on universalism and compare them with biblical teaching.

Is history tragic?

Have billions of people been created only to spend
eternity in conscious punishment and torment,
suffering infinitely for the finite sins they committed
in the few years they spent on earth?[72]

The chapter also says, "At the center of the Christian tra-
dition since the first church have been a number who insist
that history is not tragic, hell is not forever."[73]

First, the question above assumes that the human perspective on this issue determines the value of the answer. If
billions aren't saved, then history is tragic and God has failed.

This is not the first time this sort of question has been
asked. In the middle of his letter to the Romans, Paul talks
about the Jewish people's rejection of Christ. These are the
people God chose to be in a covenant relationship with and
to whom he gave so many gifts to that end. But most failed
to trust in Christ. Then Paul asks the rhetorical question,
"Well then, has God failed to fulfill his promise to Israel?"
(Romans 9:6).

He goes on to show how God takes the initiative in all
these matters, which leads to another question and another
response:

*Are we saying, then, that God was unfair? Of course
not! For God said to Moses,*

> *"I will show mercy to anyone I choose,*
> *and I will show compassion to anyone I choose."*

So it is God who decides to show mercy. We can neither choose it nor work for it.

(ROMANS 9:14-16)

In the end, Paul reminds his readers that when it comes to such inscrutable matters, we really don't know what we are talking about: "Who are you, a mere human being, to argue with God?" (Romans 9:20).

This is very much in accord with the answer God gives Job after Job's relentless questioning of God: "Do you still want to argue with the Almighty? You are God's critic, but do you have the answers?"

To which Job responds,

I am nothing—how could I ever find the answers?
I will cover my mouth with my hand.
I have said too much already.
I have nothing more to say.

(JOB 40:2-5)

Such an answer strikes at the heart of the modern mindset. We appoint ourselves not only as the masters of our fates but as the judges of all things, including the behavior of God. The Bible shows no tolerance for such questions when they are grounded in pride or insatiable curiosity. It simply refuses to answer such questions, instead pointing us toward trust in God.

Of course, since the advent of Jesus Christ, that trust

is not blind. In Jesus we've been shown a God who is not merely willful and powerful, one who can do whatever he wants, but one who works his will and power for our benefit. He is the God who has shown himself to be perfectly just and perfectly merciful. Though we should care about the fate of the unsaved, the matter of how many are saved or are not saved doesn't have to be a concern of ours. We can put that matter into the hands of a good and wise Savior.

Second, we need to understand what could be called divine math. The question about the number of the saved is similar to the question raised in the New Testament regarding the Second Coming. Many early Christians counted on it happening in their lifetime. As the decades rolled on, it was clear that Jesus had not come, so some began questioning the reliability of Jesus, the trustworthiness of God. Again, the basic question was, had God failed in his promises?

The answer Peter gives points to divine math: "A day is like a thousand years to the Lord, and a thousand years is like a day" (2 Peter 3:8). In other words, our sense of proportion about chronological time has no relationship to God's reckoning of time. Peter basically says, "You really don't understand how it works. Trust God to take care of the timing."

The same can be said of the number of the saved. A billion people is to the Lord as one, and one person as to a billion. How God understands and manages the population of heaven is not something we can possibly understand.

There is one time Scripture mentions specific numbers

regarding heaven's population, and this passage reinforces the point. We are told in Revelation that 144,000 are marked by God for salvation (see 14:1). What does this number mean? Some say it is a finite number, indicating that only a relatively small number of people are destined for eternity with God. But one other consideration is that the number itself is symbolic. The number twelve indicates fullness or completeness, as with the twelve tribes that make up all the tribes of Israel or the twelve disciples of Jesus. The idea here seems to be that those who end up with God for eternity will represent the full number God intends to be there: fullness times fullness times one thousand.

The point is that God is in charge of the demographics of heaven, and we can trust him to do what is right.

Eternal Consequences

Another assumption that troubles *Love Wins* is the idea that finite sins might have eternal consequences. But a biblical understanding of the nature of existence in God suggests a few ideas that can help us comprehend this concept.

First, a God who is eternal cannot create anything without there being eternal consequences. Once a human being has been created in the image of an eternal God, he or she cannot be uncreated by anyone. The soul has an existence that moves forward within the eternity of God. We have a finite beginning, but from that beginning forward, our lives are framed by eternity.[74] The Bible says that human life is lived, then, on one of two trajectories: toward either eternal life or eternal death. Whether you understand hell as everlasting torment or as final destruction, in either case the consequence of rejecting God is eternal.

Second, God has fashioned our lives in such a way as to show us how a momentary decision can have repercussions that last a lifetime. Take a marriage proposal—more particularly, *my* marriage proposal. In most cases, you get only one chance in life to do this right. I didn't do it right. I was so nervous and so concerned to "prove" that the marriage would work, I forgot to tell my future wife that ultimately I wanted to marry her because I loved her. I just really botched it. And now every time I hear about some other man's creative and romantic marriage proposal, I kick myself for blowing my one opportunity to do that right.

In this life there are events you can navigate only once, and the consequences are profound—like marriage, parenthood, commitment to a specific career. In this life, there are moments in which the future hangs on what is done or not done in that moment: whether to swing at a pitch with the winning run on second in the last game of the World Series, whether to say yes to the army recruiter, whether to decide to drive home on a foggy night when you've had too much to drink.

Plenty of momentary decisions have consequences that last a lifetime. Such is the nature of the reality into which we have been created. Through Scripture, God shows this aspect of earthly life to be a reflection of the bigger picture. When it comes to our entire—eternal—lives, Jesus teaches that this momentary life has an eternal trajectory, that the response we make to him has eternal consequences.

This is what gives life such a sobering and joyous texture. Our lives matter. Our actions matter. We are not a mass of protoplasm or a cosmological accident. We stand in relation to eternity.

To suggest otherwise is actually to do people a disservice. If we think that what happens in this life does not have eternal value, we get lulled into a false sense of security, and we procrastinate about the most important things: *I'll work out my salvation tomorrow, or in the next life, or maybe in the life after next.* In fact, the Bible says that "*today* is the day of salvation" (2 Corinthians 6:2, emphasis added), that the Kingdom of Heaven is at hand, and that we should repent and believe. Today is the day, this is the life, when we are invited to respond to God's gracious invitation.

This naturally drives us to a question that arises in both *Love Wins* and the minds of most Christians: what about those who die as infants or children and don't have an opportunity to respond in faith to Christ? What about those who have never heard the gospel, either before the advent of Jesus or since—people raised in cultures that have never seen a church or a Christian preacher? How are they to believe?

We so desperately want to answer these questions, but the fact is that God has not revealed what he will or will not do in these cases. Like the responses given in Job and in Romans, the answers here are beyond our human capacity. What the Bible does reveal is that God in Christ has shown himself to be perfectly just and perfectly merciful. As Jonathan Edwards puts it,

> There meet in Jesus Christ, infinite justice and
> infinite grace. As Christ is a divine person, he is
> infinitely holy and just, hating sin, and disposed
> to execute condign [deserved] punishment for sin.
> He is the Judge of the world, and the infinitely just
> Judge of it, and will not at all acquit the wicked, or
> by any means clear the guilty.
>
> And yet he is infinitely gracious and merciful.
> Though his justice be so strict with respect to all
> sin, and every breach of the law, yet he has grace
> sufficient for every sinner, and even the chief of
> sinners. And it is not only sufficient for the most
> unworthy to show them mercy, and bestow some
> good upon them, but to bestow the greatest good.[75]

And so we can trust him to do what is right and good in all things. As for us, well, he has shown us what he has done in Christ and what he calls us to do: to be reconciled to him in faith and then to take that message of reconciliation to the four corners of the earth, so that all might know of his saving love.

Back to Choice

Finally, we come to the key issue of this chapter of *Love Wins*. Again we read,

If we want hell, if we want heaven, they are
ours. That's how love works. It can't be forced,
manipulated, or coerced. It always leaves room for
the other to decide. God says yes, we can have what
we want, because love wins.[76]

In chapter 6 of this book we looked at the inherent
assumption in *Love Wins* that hell is not eternal. Now we
need to look deeper into a related assumption: that even in
hell we can still repent—make a new choice—and return to
God. In other words, freedom of choice continues to be a
reality in hell.

Now we see even more clearly why *Love Wins* is the title
and theme of the book. Love requires a free response, and
according to the book, freedom is defined as the ability to
choose to do good or evil. *Love Wins* considers the greatest
expression of love to be giving people freedom to get what
they want, to choose or reject God: "God is that loving."[77]
Love wins, then, because even if people reject God, God
lets them retain their freedom, which is the highest expression of God's love. Thus, even in hell, love wins, because
God has "lovingly" let people use their freedom to make
this choice.

According to this theology, then, what really wins is
freedom of choice. *Love Wins* exalts that very American
virtue to the highest place, making free choice *the* human
value upon which our destiny is determined. God, in the
end, stands at the gate of the New Jerusalem, "allowing

and waiting and hoping for the possibility of the reconciliation" of those who have rejected him.[78] Despite the book's
repeated assertions that God is all-powerful, he ultimately
seems rather helpless.

Or, to put it another way, in this theology it is really people
that win. People get what they want, and God does not get
what he wants.[79] People are sovereign, and God is not.

But, of course, this is precisely the opposite of biblical
teaching. In the Bible, we learn that God is sovereign over
all his creation; from beginning to end, he reigns victorious
and supreme. Thus the repeated chorus of the worshipers in
heaven:

Holy, holy, holy
is the Lord God Almighty,
who was, and is, and is to come.
(REVELATION 4:8, NIV)

Furthermore, God is the author of salvation; no one
comes to him except through his power, which is the work
of the Holy Spirit. Though some Christians differ in opinion about the place of the response of faith, all agree that it
is God who from start to finish accomplishes the work of
salvation. People do not win. Freedom does not win. God
wins.

Freedom in the Bible is not freedom to choose between
alternatives, the right to choose or not choose God. As we
noted in chapter 4, the Bible is clear that we have no such

freedom. The metaphors it uses to describe our situation—darkness, deafness, death—all suggest the impossibility of seeing or hearing God, or living in him, without a miracle.

That means that those who are separated from God in hell cannot possibly turn around and start believing. To be separated from God means to be separated from the power of the Holy Spirit, who miraculously shows us who God is and what he has done for us, and who gives us the freedom to trust in Christ. Those in hell have no freedom. They are trapped in their sins. They are destined for eternal death.

It is only the active and loving power of God and the work of the Holy Spirit that open our eyes and ears to the gospel and enable us to latch onto Jesus, our Savior. Freedom is not so much the power to choose between alternatives but the miraculous ability to trust in Christ and to live as he calls us to live. Without this freedom we simply could not do either. With this freedom we can do both—and we will do both—now and for eternity.

We began this chapter by hearing a probing question from one person about the fairness and justice of God. Let us not too sweepingly dismiss such questions. Every honest believer has them from time to time. I believe that part of the process of Christian growth involves asking the toughest questions to God and to one another—as did Job, Habakkuk, and Thomas the disciple. This is one of the ways the Holy Spirit deepens our faith, putting us in a place where we think more deeply about God. When such questions are asked in humility—like the question from Mary we noted in the first chapter—the seeds of an unshakable faith are planted within us, a faith that lies on the other side of doubt. We can allow God to take us through such times of questioning so that, like Thomas, we can say even more profoundly, "My Lord and my God!" (John 20:28).

CHAPTER 8

The Victory of a Personal God

AT THE BEGINNING OF THIS BOOK, I suggested that there is something more important than the questions we ask about God, and that is the ultimate question God asks of us: "Who do you say I am?"

This is the question Jesus poses to his disciples at a crucial phase in his ministry. As they are walking near Caesarea Philippi, he asks his disciples what people think of him. Some, they say, think he is merely John the Baptist or Elijah, two prophets whose mission was to prepare the way for the Messiah.

Then Jesus asks his disciples, "But what about you? Who do you say I am?"

Peter is the one who speaks up: "You are the Messiah" (Mark 8:27-29, NIV).

Peter understands that, though others may have an exalted view of Jesus, they don't grasp his full reality. Jesus is not merely a righteous prophet, but the Messiah himself. The fuller and thicker and more real God is to us, the fuller and thicker and more real the gospel is—and the richer our lives are.

As I said in the introduction, I am glad for the conversation that *Love Wins* has started. It is a conversation that is prompting us to think more fully and deeply about God. My concern with *Love Wins* is that its view of God is not as fully real as the God of the Bible, let alone sufficient to deal with the questions it raises. Then again, others may think the same of this attempt of mine, and that is just the nature of this kind of discussion among imperfect humans. As we engage one another fairly and frankly, though, grounding all we say in the revelation of God's Word, it is the Holy Spirit and not any one of us who will continue to lead the church into all truth (see John 16:13) and thus into a deeper knowledge of God.

In this final chapter I will sum up what I've tried to articulate in this book—a view of God that I believe is in line with the full witness of Scripture and the central affirmations of the historic Christian church—and contrast that with the main lines of argument in *Love Wins*.

God: More than an Agent

Just before I started seminary, I received an extraordinary gift. I had been serving as interim youth minister at a

Presbyterian church in Fresno, California, for a year when I was accepted to Fuller Theological Seminary. As my wife and I were getting ready to leave for Pasadena, the senior pastor presented me with a check for $500—no small sum of money in 1975. He said it was from a couple in the church who wanted to make an anonymous donation toward my education.

I was thrilled and humbled and grateful. But I was so wrapped up in my life and my future and all the possibilities that awaited me, I didn't even write a thank-you note for the pastor to pass along to this couple. It didn't occur to me to try, even through an intermediary, to establish a relationship with those generous donors.

I now realize that though I saw that church as a wonderful community, I mostly thought of it in terms of what it could do for me and my future. As a result, I missed an opportunity to show that couple how much their generosity meant to me and allow them to share in a part of my experience. Looking back, I can now see a parallel between my reaction then and the way many of us view God. Something similar to my happy yet ultimately self-centered acceptance of their gift is at work when we fail to see God as anything more than a benevolent Agent in our lives.

For most of us on most days, God is one who does things for us and for our future. He is someone who answers our prayer requests. He is someone who gives peace and joy and purpose, someone who in heaven will give us all this in spades. So it's not surprising that *Love Wins* swims in this stream; it is a natural human tendency. And it is right and true as far as it goes. It just doesn't go far enough.

Scripture says the overwhelming reason for our existence is to be in fellowship with God and with one another—as Jesus puts it, he in us and we in him. The many good things he does for us are not designed merely to make us happy but also to draw us closer to him. Today we see God's face in a mirror darkly,[80] but the joy of heaven is that we'll see God face-to-face, with immediacy and without ambiguity, in a unity that does not swallow us up but allows us to fully participate in him. This is what the Bible means when it says that God is love.[81]

Love Wins also asserts that God is love, but it is difficult to discern what exactly is meant by *love* beyond a general benevolent attitude toward people. The book sometimes connects love with the death and resurrection of Christ, but it never expands on the exact nature of those events. This is a shame, because doing so would fill the word *love* with an enormous amount of biblical content. The Bible's teaching on the Atonement exposes the radical and very personal break that sin has caused, the just consequences of that disobedience, and the extraordinary substitutionary sacrifice that reconciles us with God.

The death of Christ is a victory over the powers of evil, to be sure. But we need to recognize that the evil one is not bent merely on creating injustice and suffering on the planet but also on getting us to question, doubt, and ultimately abandon our relationship with God. The serpent's first question to the woman in Genesis is, "Did God really say . . . ?"[82] Satan's final judgment in Revelation, when he is cast permanently into the lake of fire, guarantees not only that there will be no more crying or pain but, more important, that our fellowship with God will never be broken again.

When *Love Wins* does expand on the Cross and the Resurrection, it limits their work to the defeat of injustice and their power as an example that should lead us to good works. When *Love Wins* explains the meaning of the Cross and the Resurrection in some detail, it uses an approach more reminiscent of pagan fertility religions—reducing these events to mere patterns in the cycle of death and rebirth—than of the New Testament.

As a result, the word *love* as used in *Love Wins* tends to be thin. As New Testament professor Ben Witherington has noted in his blog commentary on the book, some arguments in *Love Wins* make Rob Bell "sound more like a hopeless romantic rather than a dangerous heretic."[83]

Ironically, rather than truly affirming that God is love, *Love Wins* mostly maintains that God *gives us good things.* The book fills the vast majority of its space describing what God helps us experience and do: God is the Agent who makes us happy and fulfilled. But as I argue in chapter 2, the gospel is this and much, much more. It begins with the eternal fellowship of Father, Son, and Holy Spirit, and it ends with the eternal fellowship of God and man.

I believe the reason *Love Wins* does not actually move beyond God as Agent to God as Lover is that it simply has no role for the Holy Spirit. Although one book cannot cover every biblical theme, it is surprising that a book about God's love like *Love Wins* does not even mention the name of the Holy Spirit in its pages. It is the Spirit who convicts us of sin and leads us to righteousness. It is the Spirit who guides us into the truth of Christ. It is the Spirit who binds us to the Father and to Jesus, makes us one in fellowship, and thus helps us move beyond God as the giver of good things.

Note the way Martin Luther describes this contrast between God as mere Agent and God as Love in his commentary below on 2 Peter 1:4: "He has given us great and precious promises. These are the promises that enable you to share his divine nature."

> This is one of those apposite, beautiful, and . . .
> precious and very great promises given to us, poor
> miserable sinners: that we are to become participants
> in the divine nature and be exalted so highly in
> nobility that we are not only to become loved by
> God through Christ, and have His favor and grace
> as the highest and most precious shrine, but also to
> have Him, the Lord Himself, dwelling in us in His
> fullness.[84]

The Spirit is the very energy and activity of divine love, both to us and in us. Without the work of the Holy Spirit, we end up substituting the mere gifts of God for the gift of God himself.

Unspecific Jesus

Love Wins does say in a few places that the most glorious truth is Jesus himself, that Jesus is the center of the Good News. A great deal of what *Love Wins* says about Jesus, in fact, is spot-on and, as expected from Rob Bell, vividly put. The problem is that its discussion of Jesus never moves in the direction of increasing unity with the Father through him. Instead, it tends to point to Jesus as a talisman or an ideal. For example,

> There is a mystery,
>
> something hidden in God,
>
> something that has existed
>
> and been true and been present with, and in, God since before time,
>
> and that mystery is a someone . . .
>
> Christ.
>
> Jesus.[85]

Amen! But *Love Wins* does not go on to explain what this might mean, as Paul always does when he talks about Jesus as a mystery revealed (for example, in 1 Corinthians 1–2). In the *Love Wins* discussions of Jesus, we are never moved beyond generalities that no one could possibly disagree with: "As obvious as it is, then, Jesus is bigger than any one religion."[86]

Love Wins affirms that Jesus is the way, the truth, and the life, but it also claims that Jesus never says "how, or when, or in what manner the mechanism functions that gets people to God through him."[87] This is one of the most confounding statements in *Love Wins*, because the New Testament is replete with teachings on how people come to know God: from the various ideas of the Atonement of Christ to our response of faith.

In many passages of *Love Wins*, Jesus amounts to an icon who stands for justice, generosity, and radical inclusiveness—not the fully embodied Savior who bled and died on a cross for the sins of the world so that we might be reconciled to God, individually and in community, forever.

The Great Healer

But it's not just the full reality of Jesus Christ that is downplayed in *Love Wins*; it's also the full reality of sin. Sin may be an uncomfortable topic to ponder, but there is a reason it is discussed in the Bible so often and so frankly.

Let's say you're not feeling well—your symptoms are fatigue, nausea, and loss of appetite. You go to the doctor, who runs some tests. The doctor says not to worry because it's just a rare form of the flu, and you dutifully take the prescribed medicine. But let's say that, in fact, you have terminal cancer. The doctor withholds the bad news from you, thinking that negativity will only make things worse. And who knows, maybe the medicine will work as a placebo!

Unfortunately, many Christian preachers and teachers in

our era minimize the reality and gravity of sin. I have no doubt that they do so out of a sense of compassion—exorcising negativity from the Christian faith, giving Christians a more positive and hopeful outlook, and attracting others to Christ. But in the end, we do people a grave disservice by not telling the truth about their situation.

The Bible is utterly frank about the human plight: our situation is hopeless. It's as if we are blind or deaf or dead.[88] And this is not a disease that has come upon us against our will but a crisis we have brought on ourselves. The Bible refuses to soft-pedal the diagnosis; in fact, it tends to pull out the most dramatic language to describe it:

> *There is no one righteous, not even one;*
> *there is no one who understands;*
> > *there is no one who seeks God.*
> *All have turned away,*
> > *they have together become worthless;*
> *there is no one who does good,*
> > *not even one.*
>
> (ROMANS 3:10-12, NIV)

In addition to talking about us being dead in our sins (see Colossians 2:13; Ephesians 2:5), Paul says we are alienated from God, the source of all life and goodness and love (see Colossians 1:21). This is not exactly pleasant bedside manner, but anything less than the truth would not be truly loving. The biblical writers have the courage to face the hopelessness of our situation because they are keenly aware that Jesus, in the Cross and the Resurrection, has made it possible for us to know life and love once again—that is, to be reconciled with God.[89]

Love Wins recognizes that evil is powerful and that we need God to intervene. It acknowledges that evil lies not just "out there" but that we, too, participate in evil actions that reject the will and ways of God. It recognizes, at least in a limited way, that everyone will be held accountable for those sins. But the *Love Wins* view of sin is not nearly as radical as the Bible's, and thus it tells us we have a mild sickness when in fact what we have is terminal.

First, *Love Wins* does this by limiting sin to its horizontal dimension—sin against others. For example, in the chapter on universalism, it says, "In the end, wrongs are righted and people are held accountable for the destruction they have caused"—that is, injustice and the trampling of the innocent.[90] In the chapter on heaven, it notes that we each have to recognize "our role in corrupting this world."[91] And one would hope that all of us would confess and repent of such sins, for sins they are.

But *Love Wins* fails to acknowledge that our sin is not merely horizontal but also, and more important, vertical: "Against you, you only, have I sinned and done what is evil in your sight" (Psalm 51:4, NIV). Sin ruptures our relationship with God. It alienates us from love. It divorces us from righteousness. This is why we participate in injustice in the world—we no longer participate in the life of God.

So we cannot possibly hope to attend to the horizontal evils of our world until our life in God is restored. But that reconciliation with God and the subsequent reality of our life in God and God in us is hardly mentioned in *Love Wins*, and when it is, it is left undeveloped.

Second, because sin is mostly a horizontal affair in *Love Wins*, the solution is mostly limited to the horizontal plane as well. And because our situation is seen as ultimately not that dire, the solution is within our grasp; it's a matter of choosing God with our autonomous free will. Evil and injustice may abound on the earth, and we may participate in it from time to time, but in *Love Wins* the one thing that is not fallen, corrupt, or evil is the will. The assumption throughout is that, on our own, with no help from anyone else but ourselves, we can choose God.

As I argue in chapters 4 and 7, this is a naive view of human freedom, and it results from a view of sin that is not as radical or as truthful as the view we find in Scripture. In the Bible, the will itself is so corrupt and enslaved that it takes the power of the Holy Spirit to enable us to see what Christ has done for us and to free us to respond in faith to him.

The good news is that our salvation is not dependent on our success at making right choices—in fact, the Bible regularly reminds us that we cannot consistently make good choices with our corrupt wills. As Paul puts it, "I have the desire to do what is good, but I cannot carry it out. For what I do is not the good I want to do; no, the evil I do not want to do—this I keep on doing" (Romans 7:18-19, NIV). Instead of relying on an autonomous free will to remind us to make right choices, we can simply trust what Christ has done for us on the cross and through his resurrection.

But isn't that a choice, to trust in Christ? Yes and no. It is not even a possibility—that is, we can't even recognize what Christ has done and that he invites us to respond in faith—without the work of the Holy Spirit. So the very fact that we can apprehend all this is a gift. Furthermore, to trust in Christ means that it is not *my* trust that reconciles God to me or me to God. It is the death and resurrection of Christ that reconcile God to me, and the faith empowered by the Holy Spirit that reconciles me to God.

This is why the gospel is such good news. There are times when even the most dedicated Christian will recognize that his or her life is still in shambles, still driven by selfishness, still filled with doubt and confusion about God. At such times, panic can set in. *Am I really a Christian? Is God working in my life to bring me into deeper fellowship with him? Has God given me the gift of grace? Will I enjoy the fellowship of heaven? Do I believe enough to be saved?*

The very fact that these sorts of questions bother us at such times shows that the Holy Spirit is, in fact, working in our lives. One of the Holy Spirit's jobs is to convict the world of sin and guilt (see John 16:8). So the paradox is that when we're troubled like this, it's the very sign of God working in our lives to bring us into deeper fellowship with him.

And of course, we do *not* believe enough to be saved. Of course, selfishness rules our hearts in too many ways. Of course, we have doubts and confusion about God. It's called sin. But the gospel calls us to stop looking at ourselves—at our doubts, our sins, and our choices. The gospel says look to Christ. Don't trust in your ability to choose right or even to trust perfectly. Look to Christ, who died for sinners. Faith is the drowning man grasping the outstretched arm of his rescuer. Faith includes a human response, but it isn't the main point; the Savior is.

From Anxious Speculation to Trust

Because we can trust this Savior for salvation, we can trust him in all other spheres, especially regarding those nagging questions about divine justice.

We are free in Christ to ask any question or express any doubt. In the fellowship of the church, we should welcome people's honest concerns. We should graciously try to respond as much as we can based on what God's Word teaches. But we should draw the line at foolish talk—speculation that is contrary to Scripture or that leads people astray.

To Timothy, a young pastor, Paul writes,

> *Remind everyone about these things, and command them in God's presence to stop fighting over words. Such arguments are useless, and they can ruin those who hear them. Work hard so you can present yourself to God and receive his approval. Be a good worker, one who does not need to be ashamed and who correctly explains the*

> *word of truth. Avoid worthless, foolish talk that only
> leads to more godless behavior. This kind of talk spreads
> like cancer.*
>
> (2 TIMOTHY 2:14-17)

The problem with speculation is that it knows no bounds. The universalist idea for solving the problem of unbelief is to speculate that God will eventually win people over after they suffer enough judgment. Why would we not then postulate reincarnation, with people returning to this life again and again until they get it right? Why not suppose that all language of judgment is culturally conditioned, that in the end God doesn't judge anyone for anything? And so on.

The problem with these scenarios is that in the end we know that we've made them up to comfort ourselves in the face of life's sobering realities. When we're alone in the dark, faced with our mortality, such ideas can be of no comfort because we know where they came from.

The apparent contradictions of God's love and justice are in fact two sides of one biblical paradox. Certainly, it's a paradox we have all deeply felt. Looking at the ideas of a loving and all-powerful God and the presence of evil, we wonder how the two can possibly coexist. Looking at the idea of a loving God who calls people to believe in Jesus for their salvation and at the idea of justice, we worry about the fate of those who have never heard of him. But there are other "contradictions" that we have learned to accept in faith.

For example, the Bible doesn't explain exactly how Jesus

is both human and divine, nor how the immaterial God created a material world. It simply teaches that Jesus is both human and divine; it simply says that God, who is Spirit, created a material world. Scripture is satisfied to leave paradoxes unresolved. Likewise, it teaches that God is good and just and powerful, *and* that the world is full of evil. It does not speculate about the fate of those who have not heard of Jesus or who die before the age of accountability, as troubling as we find those questions.

The Bible simply tells us to believe and share the good news that we have come to know: that God came to us in Christ, died, was raised again to make us right with him, and calls us to be reconciled to him. We are to share that news as far and wide as we can. We can carry on in our lives of love and service assuming that God, in his mercy and justice, will address the situation of those who have not heard.

Our own faith aside, one reason we may be tempted to answer these tough questions prematurely is that we want to defend God's reputation. We feel that, if we don't answer these justice questions to the satisfaction of skeptics, well, God will have a real PR problem.

But it is not our job to shore up God's reputation. He is perfectly capable of taking care of himself. If he, in fact, thought it a serious risk to leave such questions unanswered, wouldn't he have clearly answered them in his revealed Word? The fact that he hasn't suggests he is not concerned about his public image in that regard—and that there is something more important than answering such questions.

God Wins

During the early years of the Nazi rule in Germany, many Christian leaders were killed—some in war, some while resisting Hitler. Dietrich Bonhoeffer, the German theologian famous for his radical commitment to Christ and his own courageous—and ultimately fatal—resistance to Hitler, comforted his fellow believers upon hearing of these deaths:

> Who can comprehend how those whom God takes so early are chosen? Does not the early death of young Christians always appear to us as if God were plundering his own best instruments in a time in which they are most needed? Yet the Lord makes no mistakes. Might God need our brothers for some hidden service on our behalf in the heavenly world? We should put an end to our human thoughts, which always wish to know more than they can, and cling to that which is certain. Whomever God calls home is someone God has loved.[92]

Such advice is often scoffed at as simplistic or naive. But Bonhoeffer was neither; he was one of the most profound and realistic Christian theologians of the twentieth century. In fact, Bonhoeffer is expressing a difficult but biblically informed response to our heartfelt anguish at life's apparent injustices: God is in charge; he makes no mistakes; all that he does is driven by love.

In Bonhoeffer's theology, of course, divine love is not a sentimental love but one that very much embraces justice as well. Bonhoeffer recognizes that on the cross was displayed a love that incorporates a perfect justice and a perfect mercy. And because of that, he knows that we don't have to have all our questions answered. We don't have to speculate creatively about them but instead can live in grateful trust. We can pray with the psalmist:

> LORD, *my heart is not proud;*
> *my eyes are not haughty.*
> *I don't concern myself with matters too great*
> *or too awesome for me to grasp.*
> *Instead, I have calmed and quieted myself,*
> *like a weaned child who no longer cries for its*
> *mother's milk.*
> *Yes, like a weaned child is my soul within me.*
> *O Israel, put your hope in the* LORD—
> *now and always.*
>
> (PSALM 131:1-3)

In the face of the most perplexing questions, we put our hope unswervingly in the God who came to us in Christ to die for our sins and to be raised to new life, to conquer evil, to inaugurate the new age, to reconcile us to God, and to give us the Holy Spirit. As a result, we can fellowship with one another and God in a unity we can barely imagine, and we can do so for eternity.

When God poses to us the question "Who do you say I am?" he does not leave us in the dark to guess about his character. He has revealed himself to us as a personal God—a God who wins by drawing us to himself for an eternity of extraordinary fellowship. The God of Scripture is fuller, richer, deeper, and more real than the picture painted in *Love Wins*, and that God invites us to know him as he truly is.

We trust not simply that love wins or that justice also wins. In fact, we trust not in a *that* but in a *who*. And it is the perfectly merciful and just God who wins.

Appendix 1:
Discussion Guide

ONE OF THE BENEFITS of the controversy stirred by *Love Wins* is that it has sparked dialogue about key doctrines of the Christian faith. It is healthy, both as individuals and as the church, to take time to evaluate what Scripture says about heaven, hell, and other issues raised in this book. This discussion guide is intended to direct you in studying what Scripture has to say about these issues. It can be used individually to go deeper into the topics brought up in *God Wins*, or it can be used to facilitate discussion in a group setting.

Tips for Using This Discussion Guide

- Begin and end each session in prayer, asking for the guidance of the Holy Spirit.
- Have your Bible handy to look up various Scripture passages.
- Have a Bible dictionary on hand, as many overarching biblical themes are nicely summarized in such reference works.
- Use the Opening Questions to discuss as honestly as possible how you feel and what you think about the topics addressed.

- Begin or end each session with these general
  questions about *God Wins* and the topics raised
  by *Love Wins*:

  - What do you find most interesting, surprising,
    or perplexing in the chapter(s)?
  - On what points do you agree with what *God Wins*
    states and with what *Love Wins* states?
  - On what points do you disagree?
  - What does Scripture say about the topic of this
    chapter?
  - Be sure to make time for the Scripture reading and
    discussion to keep the conversation grounded in
    biblical teaching.

CHAPTER 1: The Really Important Question

"I will climb up to my watchtower and stand at my guard-post. There I will wait to see what the LORD says and how he will answer my complaint" (Habakkuk 2:1).

Opening Questions

1. In your life, what are some of the persistent questions about life and God that bother you?

2. What questions do you have right now about the issues raised by *Love Wins*?

Read and Discuss

3. Read the stories of Zechariah and Mary and their encounters with the angel Gabriel (see Luke 1:5-24; Luke 1:26-38).

   • What are the similarities and differences in Zechariah's and Mary's encounters?

- Do you agree with the author that Mary's question was asked in faith and Zechariah's was asked in an attempt to justify himself?

- How can a question be an attempt to justify ourselves or an attempt to test God?

- How can we tell the difference in our own hearts between asking a sincere question or merely testing God?

4. Read Habakkuk 1:1-4, 12-17.

- What are the various signs of injustice that bother Habakkuk?

- What are the specific injustices that bother you today?

5. Read Habakkuk 1:5-11; 2:2-20.

    - What are the various answers God gives Habakkuk?

    - Why do those answers often fail to satisfy people? Why do we find it so hard to simply trust God in these matters?

6. Read Habakkuk 3:1-16.

    - What are the various promises that Habakkuk depends on?

    - What are some promises of Scripture we can rely on in the face of contemporary injustices?

- When is it hard for you to trust God when life feels unjust?

- What most helps you to trust God?

7. For further study:

   - Read Job 1–3; 38–42. Consider Job's plight, his complaint, the Lord's reply, and Job's final response.

   - Read Genesis 1–3. Note the questions raised about God and by God in this passage.

CHAPTER 2: Who Is This God?

"Father, I want these whom you have given me to be with me where I am. Then they can see all the glory you gave me because you loved me even before the world began!" (John 17:24).

Opening Questions

1. What is your understanding of truth? What comes to mind when someone talks about truth?

2. Why do you pursue a relationship with God? What do you expect will happen as a result of living the Christian life, or walking with God?

Read and Discuss

3. Which view of God do you naturally gravitate toward— God as Creator, God as Lawgiver, God as Lord, God as Agent, or God as Lover? Why?

4. As you consider Scripture as a whole, which view of God do you see as most central?

5. Read John 17:20-24.

   • Count the number of times the words *one* and *unity* occur in this brief passage.

   • Count the number of times the word *love* occurs.

   • Can unity occur without love? Give some examples.

   • When unity is created by love, how is it different from mere unity?

- Why is Jesus so insistent on unity—both among the disciples and between the disciples and God?

- Jonathan Edwards says, "When persons experience true comfort and spiritual joy, their joy is the joy of faith and love. They do not rejoice in themselves, but it is God who is their exceeding joy." How can God become our exceeding joy?

6. For further study:

- Read Ephesians 2:4-6; Galatians 2:20; and 2 Peter 1:3-4. Discuss how these passages emphasize our life in God and the unity we have in him.

CHAPTER 3: Becoming One Again

"God in all his fullness was pleased to live in Christ, and through him God reconciled everything to himself. He made peace with everything in heaven and on earth by means of Christ's blood on the cross" (Colossians 1:19-20).

Opening Questions

1. What emotions, images, or thoughts do you have when you consider the crucifixion of Jesus?

2. If you could describe what Jesus means to you personally with only one word or phrase, what would it be?

Read and Discuss

3. What do you see as the greatest sign that the world needs to be put right again?

4. What are some examples of people whose sacrifice for some social sin helped to bring about change? How is their dying similar to and different from Christ's death?

5. Which Atonement metaphor of Scripture is most meaningful to you in your spiritual journey?

6. Read Romans 3:9-26.

   • What does it mean that "no one is righteous— not even one"?

   • If no one is righteous, that means you, too. How does that make you feel?

- How does Christ's death deal with the human problem?

- Why is faith such a central part of the event of our salvation?

- How is faith not merely another work— something we do?

7. For further study:

- Read Isaiah 53:4-11 and Galatians 3:13. Discuss what these passages say about the doctrine of substitutionary atonement.

CHAPTER 4: The Wonder of Faith

"Anyone who belongs to Christ has become a new person. The old life is gone; a new life has begun! And all of this is a gift from God, who brought us back to himself through Christ. And God has given us this task of reconciling people to him" (2 Corinthians 5:17-18).

Opening Questions

1. Has there ever been a time in your life when you woke up to God's presence or to an aspect of God's truth in Scripture, just as the disciples on the road to Emmaus did to Jesus?

2. Have you faced a situation in your life when you felt completely helpless? If so, describe that experience and how you got through it. If not, describe how someone you know has dealt with what seemed like an impossible situation.

Read and Discuss

3. What do you think of the author's analogy of the drowning man at sea? How does it line up with God's role and our role in salvation?

4. Describe your own conversion experience. What was God's role and your role in that experience?

5. Read Luke 24:13-34.

   - God is shown here and in other Scriptures as hiding his truth from people (see also John 12:37-40). Why might God hide himself from people?

   - Do you think God does this only for a time, or can this hiding be permanent?

6. Read Acts 9:1-18.

   • Do you think Saul made a completely free choice to believe in Jesus? How much did God influence all that happened?

   • Have you, or has someone you know, had a dramatic experience of conversion? What role did the miraculous hand of God have in this conversion?

   • Why might God work so miraculously in some people's lives and so subtly in others'?

7. For further study:

   • Paul says, "I don't really understand myself, for I want to do what is right, but I don't do it. Instead, I do what I hate. . . . I know that nothing good lives in me, that is, in my sinful nature. I want to do what is right, but I can't. I want to do what is good, but I don't. I don't want to do what is wrong, but I do it anyway" (Romans 7:15-19). Some view this passage as representing our struggle before we are saved. Others say it remains true until we are transformed by Christ at the Second Coming. What is your view? How does this affect other aspects of your faith?

CHAPTER 5: The Point of Heaven

"I saw the holy city, the new Jerusalem, coming down from God out of heaven like a bride beautifully dressed for her husband. I heard a loud shout from the throne, saying, 'Look, God's home is now among his people! He will live with them, and they will be his people. God himself will be with them'" (Revelation 21:2-3).

Opening Questions

1. What was your earliest imagination of what heaven is like?

2. What is the chief way you tend to think about heaven today?

Read and Discuss

3. What aspects of earthly life do you most look forward to seeing continued and expanded in the Kingdom of Heaven?

4. Read Mark 10:17-31.

  • Do you think the rich young ruler really had kept all these commandments?

  • At first it sounds as if eternal life hinges on whether this man abandons his wealth and follows Jesus. Is it necessary to abandon wealth to follow Jesus? Are abandoning wealth and following Jesus the prerequisites to eternal life?

  • Jesus also says that it is, in fact, impossible for rich people (or anyone else) to be saved—that only God can save them. So is this parable, in the end, about our good works, or about God's power?

5. Read Revelation 21:1-27.

  • What is most striking to you about this vision of heaven?

- What is most perplexing?

- According to this passage and elsewhere in Scripture, what is the most wonderful thing about heaven?

6. Read Revelation 4:1-11.

- What strikes you about this picture of heaven?

- Some people say that worshiping God day and night will get boring. Do you think so? Why or why not?

- In what ways should our worship on earth reflect the worship we'll be performing in heaven? What might that mean for changes in your church's worship services or your personal worship?

7. For further study:

- Read Ephesians 2:1-10. Discuss the relationship between God's action in Christ and our response of faith, between faith and good works.

- Read Psalm 63:1-8. Compare the psalmist's utter devotion to God with ours on most days. Then talk about how we might grow in our devotion to God and God alone.

CHAPTER 6: Hell and Judgment

"He ordered us to preach everywhere and to testify that Jesus is the one appointed by God to be the judge of all—the living and the dead. He is the one all the prophets testified about, saying that everyone who believes in him will have their sins forgiven through his name" (Acts 10:42-43).

Opening Questions

1. What was your earliest picture of hell? What emotions did you have about the concept of hell when you were a child?

2. What is your current idea about hell? What biblical images come to your mind when you think about it? Fire? Darkness? Conscious torment? Separation from God?

Read and Discuss

3. In what sense can we experience "hell on earth" today? How is hell on earth nothing like the hell of the Bible?

4. Read Matthew 13:24-30, 36-43, 47-50; 21:33-41;
   22:1-14; 25:1-13, 31-46.

   • Does it surprise you that Jesus talks so much about
     judgment? What are the common threads in all these
     teachings?

   • Jesus talks a good deal about the judgment, but
     it's rare to hear about this topic in sermons today.
     Why do you think that is? How can we talk about
     judgment in the context of God's character—and
     without making it just a scare tactic?

5. For further study:

   • Read Luke 16:19-31. Discuss what you think is
     the message of the parable. In light of the fact that
     this is a parable about mercy, how far can we push
     the imagery to be a literal description of heaven
     and hell?

CHAPTER 7: The Bad News: Universalism

"If you confess with your mouth that Jesus is Lord and believe in your heart that God raised him from the dead, you will be saved. For it is by believing in your heart that you are made right with God, and it is by confessing with your mouth that you are saved" (Romans 10:9-10).

Opening Questions

1. Which of the following issues perplexes you most? Why?

   • The fate of those who die as infants

   • The fate of those who have never heard the name of Jesus

   • The fate of those who have heard about but rejected Jesus

- The fate of those who have heard and seem to believe and follow but whose faith is nominal

2. What is your view about universalism—the idea that everyone will eventually get to heaven? How did you come to that view?

Read and Discuss

3. The conundrum raised in this chapter—Does God get what he wants?—is not the only theological problem raised by the twin truths that God is all-powerful and God is all-loving. How, in the end, do we resolve this tension?

4. Read Revelation 14:1-5.

- How do you understand the number 144,000? Do you see it as a limited number or a symbolic number?

- Ultimately, what is more important than the number itself?

5. Read 2 Corinthians 5:14-21.

   - How does Paul express what Christ has done for us?

   - How does he describe our response of faith?

6. For further study:

   - Read John 12:44-50; 2 Peter 2:4-9; and 1 John 4:13-17. Discuss what these passages say about God's judgment. How do these truths contradict the idea of universalism?

CHAPTER 8: The Victory of a Personal God

"God is so rich in mercy, and he loved us so much, that even though we were dead because of our sins, he gave us life when he raised Christ from the dead. (It is only by God's grace that you have been saved!) For he raised us from the dead along with Christ and seated us with him in the heavenly realms because we are united with Christ Jesus" (Ephesians 2:4-6).

Opening Questions

1. Who do you say God is? What are the most important aspects of his character?

2. What questions do you still have about *Love Wins*? What key points have you taken away from this book and this study?

Read and Discuss

3. Who do you say God is? That is, what are the most important aspects of his character?

4. How is the Bible's view of love unlike a more sentimental view of love?

5. The author argues that our union with God in Christ—our intimate fellowship with the Trinity— is key to biblical salvation. Do you agree or disagree? Is this message one that is emphasized in the church today?

6. Read Romans 3:9-20.

• Why do you think Paul drives home this point in such unrelenting fashion?

• In what ways does this message bring us hope?

- What is the relationship between our sins against God and our sins against others and against God's creation? Are they equal? Does one lead to the other? Can we say that some sins are "less important" than others?

7. Read 2 Timothy 2:14-17.

- Why is Paul concerned about "worthless, foolish talk"? What makes talk worthless or foolish?

- Do the questions raised and answers given in *Love Wins* amount to foolish talk in your view? Why or why not?

- How can we tell when our speculations are driven by a desire to avoid God rather than a desire for God?

8. For further study:

- Read Psalm 131:1-3. Note all the areas where you find it hard to trust God. Then write a paraphrase of this psalm as a way to pray for more trust.

Appendix 2:
Further Reading

Atonement

Scot McKnight, *A Community Called Atonement: Living Theology* (Nashville: Abingdon Press, 2007).

McKnight likens the New Testament views of atonement to the many golf clubs needed to play a round of golf. If we use only one club, our play will be severely limited. Likewise, if we depend on only one atonement metaphor, we will fail to see the breadth and glory of Christ's salvation.

John R. W. Stott, *The Cross of Christ* (Downers Grove, IL: InterVarsity Press, 2006).

This is now considered a classic explanation of the Atonement by one of the premier evangelical Bible teachers. J. I. Packer calls it Stott's "masterpiece."

Faith

N. T. Wright, *Small Faith, Great God* (Downers Grove, IL: InterVarsity Press, 2010).

Wright reminds readers that what matters is not so much our faith itself as *who* our faith is in. Faith allows us to see our situation and our own weakness in light of God, who is powerful, holy, and loving. It's not great faith we need; it's faith in a great God.

Grace

Michael Horton, *The Gospel-Driven Life: Being Good News People in a Bad News World* (Grand Rapids, MI: Baker, 2009).

A bracing wake-up call for an American church occupied with itself, evidenced by its feverish activity and efforts at self-improvement. Horton guides readers to reorient their faith and the church's purpose toward the objective reality of what God has done in Christ.

Phillip Cary, *Good News for Anxious Christians: 10 Practical Things You Don't Have to Do* (Grand Rapids, MI: Brazos, 2010).

Cary explains that knowing God is a gradual process that comes as the Bible is read and taught in the church. He skillfully exposes our temptation to make the faith about what we feel and what we do, and he reminds readers of the good news of the gospel.

Heaven

Randy Alcorn, *Heaven* (Carol Stream, IL: Tyndale House, 2004).

Paul Enns, author of *Heaven Revealed*, sums it up best: "This is without question the most thoroughly researched, biblically oriented publication on heaven." No wonder it has sold three-quarters of a million copies.

Life in God

Donald Fairbairn, *Life in the Trinity: An Introduction to Theology with the Help of the Church Fathers* (Downers Grove, IL: InterVarsity Press, 2009).

Fairbairn mines the Bible and the teachings of the early church to remind readers of the central role of the Trinity in the life of faith—and especially how we share in the life of the Trinity through Christ.

Fred Sanders, *The Deep Things of God: How the Trinity Changes Everything* (Wheaton, IL: Crossway, 2010).

Sanders demonstrates how the Trinity is at the heart of the gospel and the foundation of the Christian life. He makes his points not only with Scripture but also by sharing the insights of distinctly evangelical authors.

Appendix 3:
Charitable Engagement

ONE THING I'VE TRIED TO MODEL in this book and in my other writings about *Love Wins* is how we might engage with those with whom we vigorously disagree. My desire is to engage charitably, but that is not the same thing as being theologically soft. Charitable and fair engagement does not require one to abandon the Bible or one's convictions. In fact, true dialogue demands that we engage one another vigorously.

But if we don't engage charitably, it calls into question the very biblical faith we are discussing. At the heart of that faith is the notion that God is gracious and patient with each of us, that he goes to extraordinary lengths to bring us into fellowship with him. The first time we have a heretical thought, God does not pronounce us heretics and dismiss us. Instead, he patiently works with us to bring us more deeply into his truth.

Besides the fact that God expects us to treat others with the charity he extends to us, we must also face this humbling fact: God also speaks to us and shapes us through those with whom we disagree. This should give us pause and help us to listen first.

It may be that a person questioning the faith is merely a skeptic trying to discredit Christian beliefs. Or we may be dealing with a person who is hurt and angry and is striking out at God in a desperate attempt to get right with him. We cannot know this in a few minutes. It takes patient listening to discern such matters. Often we will never be able to discern the deepest motives of a person's heart and can only trust that, through the bitter questions and in the ensuing conversation, the Holy Spirit is at work stirring up faith in all involved.

But the fact that we are called to listen patiently and wrestle with difficulties afresh doesn't mean we are required to dialogue *ad infinitum.* I have been a part of two mainline Protestant denominations for much of my life, both of which seem to think that dialogue is an end in itself. On many crucial issues, even after thirty years of dialogue, they are reluctant to let their yes be yes and their no be no. Certainly for individuals, and more so for churches and denominations, there comes a time to clarify and confirm exactly what we believe; for example, about the Atonement and hell. But when a book comes out that stirs up strong reactions, it becomes clear that tens of thousands of believers are wrestling with these issues. So we'd best step back, listen hard to the doubts and concerns, and take time to engage charitably.

At times like these, there arises a longing for an authoritative body to pronounce a final verdict to deal with the troublemakers by edict. But God tends to do such theological work through the church and the Holy Spirit. We believe that God is sovereign in his church, that the Holy Spirit will guide us into all truth, that through discussion and debate a sifting process will allow the truth of God in Christ to deepen and broaden.

If Jesus is truly Lord of his church, his truth will make its way into the church's life, one way or another. Our job is to prayerfully read Scripture, talk with one another from the bonds of love, and yes, state clearly what we believe, contrasting that with what we believe is inaccurate or even false teaching. I've tried to do that in this book, and I've tried to do it in a way that is fair and does not impugn motives.

This sifting process is not new; it has been happening since the beginning of the church. But we are wise not to end some conversations prematurely, especially when it may be that the Spirit is the one starting the unnerving conversations afresh in the first place.

Charitable engagement is not rocket science, but it does take intentionality. I for one need to regularly remind myself about how to do it:

1. *Try to listen carefully, and read and reread.* In conversation, I want to ask lots of questions to make sure I understand what the other person is saying.
2. *Listen in particular for the motive.* What has prompted the person's questions and concerns? The way I reply to mocking skepticism, though still respectful, is different from the way I reply to sincere questions.
3. *Aim to use the Bible as a guide to discern the truth of the person's argument—and of your own.* The Bible is

the means by which God has revealed himself to us in Christ, and the means by which the Holy Spirit continues to guide us into all truth. It remains the authoritative, infallible guide in all matters of faith and practice.

4. *Disagree with ideas, not with a person.* I try to refrain from impugning motives. I try to give credit where credit is due, noting every place of common belief.

5. *Be teachable.* It is a conversation we're in, so we can only assume that we have things to learn that can deepen our faith.

6. *Try to apply the truths of Scripture not merely as you understand them but as the historic church has held them.* I want to avoid the response, "Well, that's just your interpretation." There are matters of interpretation in which Christians of good faith can disagree. But when it comes to the substantive issues, I want to argue for "what has been believed everywhere, always, and by all."[93]

In the end, it is not our job to convince others or to justify our faith to their satisfaction, let alone to defend God's honor. Our job is to witness to what we know, and what we know has been revealed to us in God's Word through the power of the Holy Spirit. We are all called to teach what has been handed down to us (see 1 Corinthians 15:1-8), and then we let the Holy Spirit manage the results.

That is ultimately the reason we can be charitable while

being firm in our convictions. It is not our job to save the world; it is God's. Knowing this frees us from having to judge or condemn. Instead, we can simply participate with God in his patient work of bringing people—including and especially ourselves!—more and more deeply into fellowship with him.

Notes

1. See Luke 10:26-28.
2. Rob Bell, *Love Wins* (New York: HarperOne, 2011), 134, 135.
3. Ibid., 172.
4. Ibid., 198.
5. Ibid., 2.
6. C. S. Lewis, *God in the Dock* (Grand Rapids, MI: Eerdmans, 1994).
7. *Love Wins*, 172.
8. Ibid., 179–182.
9. Ibid., 178–179.
10. Ibid., 198, emphasis added.
11. Jonathan Edwards, "The Excellency of Christ" (sermon), accessed June 12, 2011, http://www.prayermeetings.org/files/Jonathan_Edwards/JE_The_Excellency_of_Christ.pdf.
12. Charles Spurgeon, "The Statute of David for the Sharing of the Spoil" (sermon, Metropolitan Tabernacle, London, June 7, 1891), accessed June 12, 2011, http://www.spurgeon.org/sermons/2208.htm.
13. Jonathan Edwards, "Love, the Sum of All Virtue" (sermon, Northampton, MA, 1738), accessed June 12, 2011, http://www.biblebb.com/files/edwards/charity1.htm.
14. See Isaiah 49:15; Ephesians 5:28-32; John 15:4-5; Job 33:4; John 4:10, 13-14.
15. *Love Wins*, 128.
16. Ibid., 129.
17. Ibid.
18. Ibid.
19. See, for example, Romans 3:25-26; Galatians 3:13; Isaiah 53.
20. *Love Wins*, 134.
21. Ibid., 39.
22. Ibid., 136.
23. Ibid., 137.
24. Ibid., 131, 136, 137.
25. H. Richard Niebuhr, *The Kingdom of God in America* (New York: Harper & Row, 1937; Middletown, CT: Wesleyan University Press, 1988), 193.

26. Jonathan Edwards, "The Excellency of Christ" (sermon), accessed June 12, 2011, http://www.prayermeetings.org/files/Jonathan_Edwards/JE_The_ Excellency_of_Christ.pdf.

27. C. S. Lewis, *Surprised by Joy* (New York: Harcourt Brace, 1955), 221.

28. *Love Wins*, 116.

29. Ibid., 116–117.

30. Ibid., 117.

31. Ibid.

32. See Genesis 27:28; Deuteronomy 28:12; Isaiah 40:26.

33. See Daniel 4:26; Matthew 4:17; Matthew 11:12.

34. See 1 Kings 22:19; Psalm 103:19; Revelation 12:10.

35. *Love Wins*, 57.

36. Ibid., 33.

37. Ibid., 34–36.

38. Ibid., 37.

39. Ibid., 39.

40. Ibid., 40.

41. Ibid., 47.

42. Ibid.

43. Ibid., 48.

44. Ibid., 50–51.

45. Ibid., 60–61.

46. Ibid., 58–59.

47. *Patton*, directed by Franklin J. Schaffner (Los Angeles, CA: Twentieth Century-Fox Film Corporation, 1970).

48. See Matthew 3:11; 10:34; John 2:15; Mark 8:34-35.

49. *Love Wins*, 64.

50. Ibid., 67.

51. Ibid.

52. Ibid., 72.

53. Ibid., 75.

54. Ibid., 88.

55. Ibid., 91.

56. Ibid.

57. Scot McKnight, "Exploring Love Wins 5," Jesus Creed (blog), April 11, 2011, http://www.patheos.com/community/jesuscreed/2011/04/11 /exploring-love-wins-5.

58. *Love Wins*, 72.

59. Ibid., 50–51.

60. See Mark 12:1-11; Luke 13:22-30; Luke 14:15-24.

61. *Love Wins*, 2.
62. Ibid., 116.
63. Ibid., 98.
64. Ibid., 107.
65. Ibid., 107, 106.
66. Martin Luther, *Works*, ed. G. Winke and H. T. Lehmann, vol. 43, *Devotional Writings* (Philadelphia: Fortress Press, 1986), 53–54.
67. *Love Wins*, 110.
68. Ibid., 99.
69. See Philippians 2:10-11.
70. *Love Wins*, 101.
71. Richard Bauckham, "Universalism: A Historical Survey," *Themelios* 4, no. 2 (September 1978): 47–54, http://www.theologicalstudies.org.uk/article_ universalism_bauckham.html.
72. *Love Wins*, 102.
73. Ibid., 109.
74. See Ecclesiastes 3:11; John 6:63.
75. Jonathan Edwards, "The Excellency of Christ" (sermon), accessed June 12, 2011, http://www.prayermeetings.org/files/Jonathan_Edwards/JE_The_ Excellency_of_Christ.pdf.
76. *Love Wins*, 118–119.
77. Ibid., 117.
78. Ibid., 115.
79. Ibid., 116.
80. See 1 Corinthians 13:12, ASV.
81. See 1 John 4:8.
82. Genesis 3:1.
83. Ben Witherington, "'For Whom the Bell Tolls . . . ' Chapter Four: Does God Always Get What He Wants?," *The Bible and Culture* (blog), March 29, 2011, http://www.patheos.com/community/bibleandculture/2011/03 /29/%E2%80%98for-whom-the-bell-tolls%E2%80%A6%E2%80%99- chapter-four-does-god-always-get-what-he-wants.
84. Quoted in Tuomo Mannermaa, *Christ Present in Faith: Luther's View of Justification* (Minneapolis: Fortress Press, 2005), 20–21.
85. *Love Wins*, 150.
86. Ibid.
87. Ibid., 154.
88. See Isaiah 42:19; Colossians 2:13.
89. See 2 Corinthians 5:18-19.
90. *Love Wins*, 112.

91. Ibid., 39.
92. Dietrich Bonhoeffer, "Circular Letter to the Confessing Churches August 1941," quoted in Eric Metaxas, *Bonhoeffer: Pastor, Martyr, Prophet, Spy* (Nashville: Thomas Nelson, 2010), 383.
93. *The Vincentian Canon*, in Commonitorium, chapter IV, 434, Cambridge Patristic Texts.

Acknowledgments

A book of this nature—a "rapid response" book—does not come about except for the hard and quick work of many people. I thank . . .

David Neff, my boss at *Christianity Today*, for giving me space to write a number of online commentaries on *Love Wins*, which helped me shape this response,

Jim Bell, for suggesting my name to Tyndale as the author for this project,

Jon Farrar, who steadily guided the vision for the book through all the Tyndale editorial meetings,

Stephanie Voiland, whose encouragement and expert edits improved the manuscript from cover to cover,

And Barbara, my wife, who let me off the hook from all family chores while I wrote this book!

About the Author

MARK GALLI was born and raised in California, received his BA in history from UC Santa Cruz and an MDiv from Fuller Theological Seminary, and did some doctoral work at UC Davis. He served as a Presbyterian pastor for ten years—four in Mexico City and six in Sacramento—before becoming a journalist. He has spent twenty-two years as an editor with the following magazines: *Leadership*, *Christian History*, and *Christianity Today*. Mark has been interviewed on numerous radio shows over the years and has been quoted in the *New York Times*, the *Wall Street Journal*, *Time*, and *Newsweek*, among others. He has been married to his wife, Barbara, for thirty-six years; has three grown children; and currently lives in Glen Ellyn, Illinois.

MORE BOOKS FROM MARK GALLI

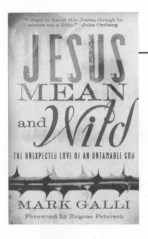

Jesus Mean and Wild

In this book, Mark shows us that Jesus is not as "meek and mild" as we are sometimes led to believe. By examining the Gospel of Mark, he explains how the bracing words and actions of Jesus are actually demonstrations of his love.

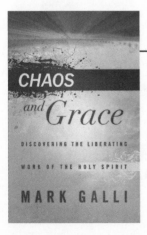

Chaos and Grace

We work to control our time, our TVs, our weight, and even our faith lives. But all that control, we soon find out, is exhausting. *Chaos and Grace* offers readers freedom by reintroducing them to the liberating work of the Holy Spirit—which often comes to us through crisis.

Releases October 2011

CP0498

SOULWORK is a biweekly column at ChristianityToday.com, where Mark discusses the implications of the Christian faith for our lives and our churches.

 Visit http://www.christianitytoday.com /ct/features/opinion/columns/markgalli or scan the QR code.

CP0499